Cambridge Studies in Management

13

Managing owners

The National Freight Consortium in perspective

Cambridge Studies in Management

Formerly Management and Industrial Relations series

Editors

W I L L I A M B R O W N *University of Cambridge*
A N T H O N Y H O P W O O D, *London School of Economics*
and P A U L W I L L M A N, *London Business School*

The series focuses on the human and organisational aspects of management. It covers the areas of organisation theory and behaviour, strategy and business policy, the organisational and social aspects of accounting, personnel and human resource management, industrial relations and industrial sociology.

The series aims for high standards of scholarship and seeks to publish the best among original theoretical and empirical research; innovative contributions to advancing understanding in the area; books which synthesize and/or review the best of current research, and aim to make the work published in specialist journals more widely accessible; and texts for upper-level undergraduates, for graduates and for vocational courses such as MBA programmes. Edited collections may be accepted where they maintain a high and consistent standard and are on a coherent, clearly defined, and relevant theme.

The books are intended for an international audience among specialists in universities and business schools, undergraduate, graduate and MBA students, and also for a wider readership among business practitioners and trade unionists.

Other books in the series:

Managing owners

The National Freight
Consortium in perspective

KEITH BRADLEY

and

AARON NEJAD

The London School of Economics and Political Science
Business Performance Group

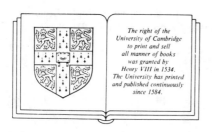

The right of the
University of Cambridge
to print and sell
all manner of books
was granted by
Henry VIII in 1534.
The University has printed
and published continuously
since 1584.

CAMBRIDGE UNIVERSITY PRESS
Cambridge
New York   Port Chester
Melbourne   Sydney

Published by the Press Syndicate of the University of Cambridge
The Pitt Building, Trumpington Street, Cambridge CB2 1RP
40 West 20th Street, New York, NY 10011, USA
10 Stamford Road, Oakleigh, Melbourne 3166, Australia

First published 1989

Printed in Great Britain at the University Press, Cambridge

British Library cataloguing in publication data

Bradley, Keith, 1944–
  Managing owners: The National Freight
  Consortium in perspective.–(Cambridge
  studies in management)
  1. Great Britain. Companies. Industrial
  relations. Effects of ownership of shares by
  personnel
I. Title II. Nejad, Aaron
331

Library of Congress cataloguing in publication data

Bradley, Keith.
  Managing owners: the National Freight Consortium in perspective/
  Keith Bradley and Aaron Nejad.
  p. cm. – (Cambridge studies in management: 13)
  Bibliography
  Includes index.
  ISBN 0 521 36023 4
  1. National Freight Consortium. 2. Employee ownership – Great
  Britain – Case Studies. I. Nejad. Aaron. II. Title. III. Series.
  HE5663.Z7N383 1989
  388′.044′06041–dc20 89-7282 CIP

ISBN 0 521 36023 4

AN

To the memory of Avram

Contents

Contents

Tables

Figure

Acknowledgements

During the period we researched this work the investigation of employee financial participation was regarded as marginal to the interests of mainstream industrial relations specialists. As a result, our research met with both encouragement and hostility. Both served to strengthen our resolve. In particular, we thank senior management and employees at the National Freight Consortium whose cooperation brought this study to life. The study also benefited from discussions with trade unionists, members of financial institutions and others. Willie Brown and Nancy Jackson made valuable comments on the drafts. Trisha Hammond provided excellent back-up in preparing the manuscript.

Abbreviations

AUEW	Amalgamated union of Engineering Workers
BMB	Barclays Merchant Bank
BREPS	British Railways Express parcels Service
BRS	British Road Services
BTC	British Transport Commission
The Consortium	National Freight Consortium
ESOP	Employee Stock Ownership Plan
NFC	National Freight Company
	National Freight Corporation
NUR	National Union of Railwaymen
SAYE	Save-As-You-Earn Share Option Scheme
RHE	Road Haulage Executive
Schroders	J. Henry Schroder Wagg
TGWU	Transport and General Workers Union
THC	Transport Holding Company
TSSA	Transport Salaried staff Association
TUC	Trade Union Congress
URTU	United Road Transport Union

1

The emergence of employee ownership

Introduction

Historically the study of industrial relations has tended to concentrate on collective bargaining and the agencies associated with those endeavours. During the post-war era of industrial expansion in large-scale, labour-intensive, unionised manufacturing industry, academic interest in labour relations grew but continued to focus primarily on the rules of collective bargaining, from the origins of the trade union movement in the struggles of craft workers to maintain privilege, to unionism in its mature phase. This emphasis has important practical implications. It perpetuates the antagonistic model of labour–capital relations, with its overtones of class struggle, and causes alternative models of industrial relations to be dismissed out of hand as impractical or applicable only in very unusual circumstances.

Now, however, the old boundaries of the discipline of industrial relations begin to blur as academic commentators react to changes in the economy. The density of unionism is shrinking, organising costs are rising, there are signs that the labour movement is re-evaluating its role and some unions are actively promoting a less adversarial position in collective bargaining. In addition, companies are considering initiatives which they hope may reduce the importance of labour relations processes based on the institutions of collective bargaining, or at least transform the character of such bargaining. The public pronouncements of some corporate leaders suggest that top management may now be persuaded that productive efficiency depends on transforming low-trust employee relations into ones of high trust. One way of encouraging this shift is to introduce an element of employee ownership which will restructure incentives at the level of the firm and bring the interests of management and workers closer together. Little research has been done to explore the role of employee share ownership in fostering harmonious industrial relations. Indeed, there has been little coherent academic treatment in Britain of companies where profit-sharing plans appear to be the norm rather than the exception.

Traditional industrial relations emphasise bargaining modes which favour wage rigidity and hinder more general labour flexibility. From here it is but a short step to macro-economic imbalance, Keynesian demand stimulation and the accumulation of inflationary forces, as a major segment of the economy attempts to insulate itself from adverse shocks or to further its own living standards through monopsony. The great significance of employee ownership is that it moves away from the fixed-wage residual-profit bargain.

This book examines one of the most significant cases of employee share ownership in Britain and assesses its impact upon traditional industrial relations. The National Freight Consortium (NFC) is the largest and most diverse road freight transport, storage and distribution company in Britain, with interests in the travel business and property management. In February 1982, during the early stages of the British government's privatisation programme, the former National Freight Corporation[1] was bought by an employee consortium, the National Freight Consortium, for £53.5 million. Since this historic purchase, the NFC's performance has been outstanding; a stagnating nationalised industry appears to have been converted rapidly into a highly efficient and growing road transport-based group. The Conservative government depicts the NFC as an eloquent illustration of the merits of both privatisation and employee share ownership. In FY 1987–8 the company made operating profits of £90.4 million from a turnover of £1.26 billion. Currently over 80 per cent of its 32,000 employees together with a further 18,000 former employees, relatives and pensioners, own more than 83 per cent of the company's equity. Indeed the NFC has become the largest industrial enterprise of its kind in Europe.

Privatisation and employee ownership

To understand the particular model of ownership adopted by the NFC it is helpful to distinguish four types of employee ownership: (i) profit-sharing and employee share schemes, (ii) management and employee buyouts, (iii) producer cooperatives, and (iv) industrial partnerships.

As a result of tax inducements initiated in the Finance Act 1978 and 1980, the number of *profit-sharing* and *savings-related share option* schemes has grown steadily. By 1989 there were some 780 approved profit-sharing schemes and 787 savings-related share option schemes which are estimated to cover nearly 3 million employees.[2]

The approved schemes work as follows. In an approved profit-sharing scheme under the Finance Act 1978 a company channels a certain percentage of its profits, usually not more than 5 per cent, into a trust.[3] The trust then purchases shares in the company and allocates them to eligible employees. If an employee retains his shares for a sufficient period, specified in the Finance Act and currently five years, he is exempt of income tax and capital gains tax. The company may offset the costs of the scheme against any corporation tax liability.[4]

The approved savings-related share option scheme introduced under the Finance Act 1980 requires an employee to take out a standard Save-As-You-Earn (SAYE) contract, which binds him to save up to a maximum of £100 a month for either five or seven years. When the contract expires the employee may purchase the company's shares. The price of the shares to be bought is specified when the contract is taken out, but with a maximum discount of 10 per cent on the prevailing price at the time. The employee is exempt of income tax on any capital gains if the option is exercised.[5]

Since the late 1970s, management and employee *buyouts* have emerged as a novel form of employee share participation. In these deals a corporation, or one of its subsidiaries, is acquired by employees involved in running the company, usually a consortium of managers. Between 1980 and 1987 some 1,500 buyouts occurred in Britain when previously only some five to ten cases had been recorded each year. The size of management buyouts has also increased during this period. In 1985 there were 33 deals of over £5 million against an average in 1979 of £0.5 million. During 1979–87 the total annual value of management buyouts increased from £50 million to over £3 billion.

As with employee share schemes, several different structures of buyout are possible. Rarely does a consortium take all of the equity. In many cases, majority ownership of the new company rests with a consortium whilst any balance may be taken by financial institutions. Although buyouts are employee-owned firms in the sense that those involved in the company may own a substantial proportion of the firm's equity, they often bear closer resemblance to partnerships in the professions. This is particularly true of management buyouts. Control is based on equity ownership, and democratic institutions for decision-making do not necessarily exist; there are no restrictions on the return to capital or on how profits are distributed, except those which may be imposed by creditors. Channels of communication with employees may be improved, but equity participation is not usually extended to rank and file workers. Furthermore, the company culture resembles that of a conventional business organisation.

The *producer cooperative* sector has traditionally been small in Britain. From 1975 to 1978 the number of producer cooperatives increased ninefold from 20 to 180. The Cooperative Development Agency (CDA)

3

estimate that there are currently over 1,400 cooperatives in Britain employing between 2 and 500 people each, for a total of over 10,000 people. The overall impact of producer cooperatives therefore has remained small. However, European studies have suggested that cooperatives have a faster rate of employment creation than conventional companies, so that their significance for public policy may continue to grow (Estrin, 1985).

Although cooperatives take different forms, most share some fundamental principles. Membership is based on employment which is open and voluntary. Non-membership labour is eschewed. Control is based on the principle of one-person-one-vote, irrespective of an individual's capital or labour input. Some cooperatives permit their members to make capital investments in the organisation so that large individual interests in the enterprise do occur. But a fixed rate of return is paid on all share capital. Profits are then divided among the members in an equitable way.

Industrial partnerships are far fewer in number than orthodox producer cooperatives, but they often employ many more people. In this respect the partnership sector is much larger than the producer cooperative sector. For example, the John Lewis Partnership (JLP) employs some 30,000 people, about three times the number in the entire orthodox producer cooperative sector.

Like orthodox producer cooperatives, industrial partnerships are characterised by membership based on employment and a democratic organisational structure based on the one-person-one-vote principle. But partnerships have three distinguishing characteristics. Firstly, the organisation is normally socially owned in a trust.[6] Individuals usually have no personal shareholding although they may participate in profit-sharing and decision-making. Secondly, employees are less likely to think of themselves as part of a partnership or cooperative. Employees are encouraged to participate in the trust's decision-making process and other activities, but participation is not compulsory or expected. Thirdly, industrial partnerships tend to be formed where the previous owners themselves have decided to transfer the company. Owners may choose to set up an employee trust for various reasons: a philosophical commitment to employee ownership; the desire to avoid a succession problem; or the desire to realise the value of a private company without relinquishing full control.

Interest in employee ownership started earlier and has had a greater impact in the United States. A series of federal laws since the 1970s has encouraged the growth of Employee Stock Ownership Plans (ESOPs). By 1986, the National Center for Employee Ownership estimated that some 8,000 ESOPs covering 11 million workers or 8 per cent of the workforce existed in the United States.[7] Growth has also been quick in Britain.

Between 1978 and December 1988, the number of share-based profit-sharing and employee share schemes increased from 30 to over 1,500; nearly 3 million employees are currently covered. Over a similar period employee buyouts also increased significantly, and producer cooperatives and industrial partnerships increased nearly tenfold to over 2,000 recorded cases, employing 17,000 people. After the introduction of Profit Related Pay in 1987, 430 schemes covering some 73,000 employees had been organised by January 1988. (Over 25,000 enquiries were made, so the take-up rate was low.)

In the late 1970s, Britain's competitive crisis encouraged management in the private sector to redouble its pursuit of productive efficiency. This effort included a reconsideration of the organisation and motivation of labour, with particular attention to the role of employee share ownership. At the same time, the role of the state in industrial relations was under challenge. The competitive crisis also threatened public finance. Some economists attributed the British economy's decline to the high levels of public expenditure, which diverted resources from more productive sectors (Bacon and Eltis, 1978). In 1979 the newly elected Conservative government began a radical programme to reduce the activities of the public sector, and privatisation emerged as a significant part of government policy.

To date, the record of the privatisation of state enterprises has been impressive and represents an important shift in the ownership of British industry. Between 1979 and 1988 the British government received some £25 billion from sales of state enterprises. So far 13 listed companies have been created with a market value of some £50 billion. The proportion of the Gross Domestic Product attributable to state-owned companies has fallen from 9 to about 5.5 per cent, and almost 1 million jobs have been transferred to the private sector.

This programme has stimulated the growth of employee ownership. In those privatised companies which have been publicly floated, a proportion of the new company's ordinary share capital has typically been reserved by the government for eligible employees. The sale of the main privatised enterprises to date has created some 700,000 employee-shareholders. These companies may operate approved schemes under the Finance Act but most of their employee shareholding came about at the time of the transfer of ownership. Typically the workforce was offered shares in them on favourable terms.[8]

There have also been several successful employee and management buyouts from state enterprises. They have been mainly management buyouts of subsidiaries of the nationalised industries. For example, 20 subsidiaries of the National Bus Company were sold this way. Victualic

5

Engineering in the steel industry which employs some 1,000 people is another thriving example. The much larger buyout at Vickers/Cammell Laird which employs 14,000 has been unsuccessful. The buyout option was also discussed in other privatisations including Jaguar Cars, British Transport Hotels and British Airways. But the NFC case is unique: an entire nationalised industry with a workforce in 1982 of some 23,500 was sold to an employee consortium. Further, as the phenomenon of privatisation spreads around the world, there are indications that employee and management buyouts are often either considered or are taking place (Letwin, 1988).

Objectives of the study

This study employs data from the NFC in order to achieve three main objectives. Firstly, the NFC experience illuminates the changing political, economic and managerial environments and their impact on industrial relations. Despite the growth in employee ownership, relatively little work has been done to investigate its nature and effects. A pioneering attempt was made by Bradley and Gelb (1983a) who suggested that the employee buyouts of the 1970s were responses to industrial restructuring and plant closures in the private sector. Buyouts could be the only way to maintain a plant thereby preserving employment. They placed their analysis of this phenomenon in the context of industrial policy, and argued that the traditional post-war industrial policy in this area has been statist and interventionist. However, increasing international competition and shrinking public sector resources increasingly have constrained traditional forms of intervention, including the role of social insurer. An effective alternative form of industrial policy was to encourage employee or community responses to plant closures, assisted by either tax breaks or initial public finance.

This book has its origins in the Bradley and Gelb tradition. However, it seeks to develop these themes into a previously uncharted area: employee ownership in privatisation of state industries. The NFC case may help us to understand the process of privatisation and the buyout phenomenon, and to examine managerial efficiency and shareholder monitoring in a conversion from public to employee ownership.

Secondly, a full understanding of the process of conversion and the structure of ownership and control at the NFC may inform current public policy debates about: (i) the encouragement of employee share schemes and profit-related pay, and (ii) achieving a wider dispersal of ownership of productive assets.

In Britain, the recent increase in the number of employee share schemes has been promoted by changes in taxation and company law. Governments, managements and financial institutions increasingly have come to view employee financial participation as one response to a number of economic problems. Emphasis has shifted towards supply-side policies which affect the workings of the labour market. Initially, the focus was upon employee share schemes and how employee ownership assuages the conflict between capital and labour, harmonising labour relations and subsequently improving labour productivity and firm performance. The focus switched to profit-related pay in the Chancellor's Budget speech of March 1986, and subsequent Green Paper (1986) and White Paper and Finance Act 1987. In comparison with employee share schemes, linking pay more closely to profits was expected to have stronger and more immediate effects on the rigidity of the pay system, with benefits for employment. In addition, the scheme could be adopted more widely by unincorporated firms with no shares to issue.

An important part of the government's policies is the attempt to widen the ownership of British industry. The privatisation programme has encouraged investment by employees and private shareholders. Employee buyouts offer the opportunity to widen ownership even further. The average total employee shareholding in conventionally privatised firms after initial quick capital gains have been realised is some 3 per cent of ordinary share capital (Trades Union Congress, 1985). At the NFC, the figure at the time of privatisation was 82.5 and had increased to 83 per cent. In addition, buyouts offer the opportunity to extend privatisation into state enterprises which would otherwise be difficult to sell, dispersing productive assets which might have otherwise remained concentrated in state ownership.

Predictions about privatisation and employee share ownership may have fuelled a trend in public policy, but on a number of key issues there is a dearth of theory and empirical evidence with which to evaluate the predicted outcomes. In addition, most of the evidence that does exist is from the United States; translating these findings into a specifically British context is problematic.[9] The NFC experience provides an invaluable opportunity to fill in these gaps. In particular we address three issues:

(i) Why do buyouts occur in some cases of privatisation? We are beginning to understand the evolution of privatisation, but know less about the distribution of ownership to include a wide spectrum of employees. This study attempts to explain the motives of the main parties in buyouts from the public sector, and in particular those of a government and a buyout consortium.

(ii) Why do employees invest in their own company? Given a successful buyout attempt, why do some employees invest in conversions while others do not? Advocates of employee ownership assume that employees are willing to be used as a source of equity capital either in a buyout or in an employee share scheme. Internalising capital in this way may be beneficial to an economy during times of high interest rates, capital shortages and pressure on government expenditure, and policy-makers and managers may wish to spread risks and capital by doing so. However, a number of constraints may exist, including resistance by a labour force traditionally averse to concentrating financial risk.

(iii) What are the effects of conversion to employee ownership upon industrial relations? Advocates of employee ownership have argued that productive efficiency could be raised by raising the level of trust. Russell (1985) suggests that employee ownership has an important effect on industrial relations. As a result of closer links with the firm and democratic institutions, employee ownership could stimulate a favourable climate of industrial relations. The assumption is that employee ownership somehow improves links between the employee and the organisation. But there is little formal theory on the mechanisms by which employee share ownership affects industrial relations.

This book attempts to develop the theory. Empirical evidence is unfortunately scanty. Investigation has proceeded steadily in North America, but is almost non-existent in Britain. There have been numerous different experiments involving some element of employee financial participation. Causal circumstances and structures of ownership and control differ from case to case. Therefore generalisations from any one form of employee ownership to another should be treated with caution. This limits the value of the literature to date.

The NFC case can inform about all these issues. It represents a specific model of employee ownership, so a close analysis may provide comparisons with other major employee-owned organisations, including the John Lewis Partnership in Britain and the Mondragon system of cooperatives in Spain. Further, Britain has few employee-owned firms but cautious comparisons can be made between the individual shareholdings of NFC employees and more widespread forms of employee financial participation. Finally, the NFC may provide invaluable insights into the wider problems relating to conversions to employee ownership as it bears many of the characteristics of traditional post-war British industry, including high unionisation and traditional collective bargaining. If collective bargaining continues after a conversion, how is it affected?

Organisational structure of the NFC

The National Freight Company plc is owned by the National Freight

Consortium (the consortium) and is now known as the NFC plc. Shares in the consortium are individually owned, as in a conventional joint-stock enterprise, rather than owned by a collective trust, as in many other employee-owned firms. Early in 1988 the employee shareholders voted in favour of the company's flotation which took place early in 1989. Before flotation the consortium was structured so that shares could not be traded on the open market. Thus, the 83 per cent of the share capital was confined to a well-defined group: employees, managers, ex-employees, pensioners and their families. The flotation was designed to ensure that, assuming employees did not immediately 'stag' their shares, majority control and ownership would remain with the NFC's employees.

This meant that between privatisation and flotation the NFC had to devise new institutions and mechanisms for marketing and valuing shares while retaining the incentives of individual employee share ownership and control and a conventional management structure. The consortium's solution was based on an independent share trust. The NFC Share Trust Ltd administered the share trust as its sole trustee; its directors were appointed by the consortium. All dealings between buyers and sellers were handled by the share trust, and were restricted to four dealing days a year, chosen by the share trust. This ensured that shares moved only within the permitted circle. The price of shares and dividend payments were fixed by shareholders on recommendation of the board. In turn the board took advice from independent external accountants who made their valuations in accordance with established procedures for the valuation of unquoted shares. The accountants consulted a committee which included members of the NFC board.

Dealing was possible only if buyers and sellers could be matched at the set transfer price. To facilitate the matching, the trust held a small float of shares to clear the market on dealing days.[10] The share trust could also apply to the consortium to issue new shares. Since the numbers of buyers and sellers were unlikely to be equal under such a system at a given price, this facility was necessary, although probably not sufficient. Consequently, the share trust was permitted to publish a priorities list of preferred buyers and sellers. Had the consortium not decided to obtain a Stock Exchange listing the share trust might eventually have faced a situation where an imbalance between buyers and sellers could not be cleared. Then if the company was performing well, existing employees would be reluctant to sell; if the company performed badly, employees would find it difficult to sell out. Such problems could have threatened the NFC's viability by making it difficult for new entrants to buy in.[11] Survival as an employee owned and controlled company after flotation may also be difficult. Employees anxious to realise their capital gains may cash in their shares, and therefore lose what control they had.

Despite its ownership, the NFC's corporate structure is similar to that of a typical decentralised capitalist enterprise. There are no worker-directors on the NFC Board although a shareholder-director has been appointed since 1985. Executive directors are appointed or re-elected by the consortium at Annual General Meetings. At the operational level, subsidiaries with common activities are organised into a number of groups whilst the individual trading names and operational management of each subsidiary are retained. For example, the parcels delivery components are grouped together under a Parcels Group. Within each subsidiary there may be several locations. Typically, each location is a profit centre and retains operational control. Budgets, targets and investment decisions, motivated by commercial objectives, are set after negotiations with an organisational tier immediately above.

Although the NFC has maintained a conventional management structure, it employs a participatory style of management. Special emphasis is placed on communicating information downwards to the blue-collar majority of the workforce and involving them in decisions. The system of employee remuneration is similar to that of the rest of the industry. Employees are not obliged to make a capital investment in the NFC, nor does a capital investment guarantee employment. There are various company profit-sharing schemes, and salaries and wages can be supplemented in some locations by cash bonuses linked to performance. An employee who leaves the company is not required to sell back his purchased shares. Officially, shareholdings are secret so that the NFC's operational management does not know which employees are members of the consortium. The register of shareholders is held by the NFC share trust.

The NFC recognises a number of trade unions, including the Transport and General Workers' Union (TGWU), the Transport Salaried Staff Association (TSSA), the United Road Transport Union (URTU), the National Union of Railwaymen (NUR) and the Amalgamated Union of Engineering Workers (AUEW). Union density is very high among manual employees as the NFC operates a post-entry closed shop. Moreover, as many as 85 per cent of unionised manual employees are members of one union, the TGWU.

A formal structure of collective bargaining, joint consultation and disputes resolution exists. There are no longer any national negotiations but a Joint Negotiating Committee works at the group level; and joint committees are active at company and local levels. In the late 1970s, the negotiations over pay and conditions were devolved to the group organisational level (i.e. the Joint Negotiating Committee). This change was made in conjunction with other attempts to relate pay more closely to performance. Company Joint Committees and Local Joint Committees deal with company and branch-specific issues including company and local bonus schemes. The same machinery is used for joint consultation and grievances.

Organisation of the book

The experience of the NFC illuminates some of the important issues surrounding employee ownership. Here we examine three major questions, in each case devoting one chapter to a theoretical discussion and another to the findings of our study of the NFC. What motivates privatisation, and what determines the form it will take? (Chapters 2 and 3.) What determines whether an individual employee decides to invest in his company when he has the opportunity? (Chapters 4 and 5.) How does employee ownership influence industrial relations? (Chapters 6 and 7.) Conclusions are presented in Chapter 8.

2

Privatisation and employee ownership: issues

Introduction

Why have some privatisations of state enterprises resulted in management or employee buyouts? Since privatisation is a relatively new experience in Britain, there is little formal theoretical or empirical research to explain why employee share ownership accompanies most privatisations, or why some sales have resulted in employee buyouts.

Employee buyouts in the private sectors in both Britain and the United States have attracted a considerable theoretical and empirical analysis. Theoretically, buyouts have been viewed primarily as a response to market forces in mature industrial economies.[1] Although the immediate reasons for a buyout relate to the circumstances of the enterprise concerned, those circumstances are influenced by the prevailing economic, financial and political environments. This gives rise to two questions. Firstly, what market forces lead to divestments and closures – and hence, sometimes, to buyouts? Secondly, when management and employee buyouts result, why are those forms preferred to more conventional sales?

The following section considers why divestments occur in the private sector. However, direct inferences from the private to the public sector should be viewed with caution. Governments have distinctive interests and are subject to distinctive pressures; to some extent they may be shielded from the market forces that dominate private corporations. Similarly, once a decision to sell has been made, governments and private corporations are likely to encounter quite different environments surrounding the negotiations of a buyout. To explain why buyouts (or indeed any share ownership for employees) occur in privatisations, an understanding of the reasons for privatisation is first required.

Although the literature on privatisation is growing, it has tended to be descriptive and prescriptive, or has evaluated the relative merits of public and private ownership in a general way. Notable recent exceptions include

Vickers and Yarrow (1988) and Veljanovski (1987). To date, no attempt has been made to explore the dynamic forces of the privatisation programme in a way that sheds light upon the reasons for buyouts or share ownership for employees. We address the problem here, evaluating the debate surrounding public and private ownership, and the economic and political forces that impelled some current policy-makers towards privatisation as a strategy. Privatisation is seen as the result of various economic and non-economic factors. In the following section, we examine literature relating to private sector buyouts for insights into why buyouts from the public sector occur.

Buyouts in the private sector

In the private sector, corporations may divest parts of their business for a variety of reasons, either cyclical or structural. An internal buyout (by management or employees) is favoured when a firm would find it difficult to raise external equity capital or wishes to conclude a sale quickly.

Three main explanations have been developed for corporate divestment in the private sector: (i) both divestments and acquisitions are part of the dynamic process in capitalist economies; (ii) divestments are a response to a downswing in the business cycle; and (iii) divestments are a response to structural changes in the corporate economy. Support exists for all three explanations, although the most important explanation may be structural.

Divestments may often be part of the dynamics of the corporate economy. A corporation may shed unwanted parts of a recent acquisition. Alternatively, if a subsidiary no longer fits with the parent's mainstream activities, the corporation may reorganise the asset portfolio. The employee buyout phenomenon cannot be explained by divestments for these reasons, however.

Corporate divestment may also be due to a downturn in the business cycle. As demand contracts, profits shrink and corporations may be obliged to rationalise by shedding their less profitable units. In some cases, plants may have to be closed. If at the same time a government is eager to control the rate of price inflation by constraining monetary growth, then high interest rates may compound the problem. In this event corporations with diminishing profits may choose to relax their cash flow problems by divesting (Arnfield et al., 1981).

The British recession of the early 1980s provided some evidence to support this theory. There were some 12,500 company liquidations in England and Wales on average each year during 1980–5, more than double the corresponding number for the period 1975–9. Similarly, the average annual number of bankruptcies increased by over 20 per cent (to some 6,200) in the period 1980–5 from 1973–9.[2] Wright and Coyne's (1985: p. 68) survey of 111 British management buyouts revealed that 18 per cent resulted from either an independent or parent company in receivership. Cyclical factors clearly have influenced many insolvencies, some of which included profitable or potentially profitable units.

On the other hand, neither the number of insolvencies nor the number of buyouts decreased as the business cycle swung round after 1983. As a result, it seems likely that the recession in Britain accelerated the pace of management buyouts, but it was not 'fundamental to the phenomenon' (Economist Intelligence Unit, 1984: p. 2). Indeed, the high number of profitable subsidiaries which have been divested suggests that divestment has often occurred for structural reasons. For example, parents of firms in declining markets with low profits may conclude their 'endgame strategy' with divestment (Harrigan, 1980). Similarly, a subsidiary may require new investment which the parent prefers to allocate elsewhere. In the United States, corporate divestment has been associated with the deindustrialisation of the traditional industrial centres as a response to technological and product market changes. Firms have been taking the opportunity to relocate capital to other parts of America where unit labour costs and corporate taxation may be lower (Bluestone and Harrison, 1982).

A second structural reason for divestment may be demergers, or a reversal of the trend towards corporate acquisition during the 1960s and 1970s (Arnfield et al., 1981; Economist Intelligence Unit, 1984; and Wright and Coyne, 1985). The intensive merger activity of that period can be viewed as part of the evolution of the mature industrial economies during a period of modernisation and relatively high economic growth. Competition in expanding markets encouraged corporate growth as it enabled higher levels of investment and the advantages of economies of scale, and attracted better-quality management.

The costs of internal organisation were reduced further by the contemporary popular belief in large units of production which was reflected in government industrial policy (Cosh et al., 1980; Economist Intelligence Unit, 1984). The enforcement of the Monopolies and Mergers Act 1965 and the Fair Trading Act 1973 has been particularly lenient. During 1965–74, only 35 out of 1,038 mergers which affected the public interest were reported to the Monopolies and Mergers Commission (Cosh et al., 1980: p. 231). The feeling was that mergers were generally beneficial, and that a minister should not bar a particular merger without showing that it threatened the public interest.[3] In the United States, by contrast, the burden of proof lay with a merging group to demonstrate that an acquisition was safe. As a result the concentration of industry went further in Britain than in other industrial countries.[4]

14

By the 1980s, a different set of conditions superseded the combination of economic factors and government support which had encouraged corporate growth in the 1960s and 1970s. Low economic growth and profits replaced high economic growth and profits. The then fashionable preference for large-scale units of production had been replaced by a new emphasis on entrepreneurialism and small businesses. The economies of scale expected from large-scale production may have been offset by certain diseconomies, in particular by managerial diseconomies. Centralisation may have represented an over-emphasis on capital rather than human resources. Management's natural limitations may have been stretched which led to a reduction of control over the production process and a diminution of the incentive to maximise productive efficiency. Consequently, some mergers may have resulted in disappointing performance. Many showed poor profits, productivity and employment creation, and often worse labour relations (Meeks, 1977).[5]

Given a decision to divest, what method will be chosen? A division (or an entire corporation) could be sold to an independent external buyer. Under what circumstances is a management or employee buyout more likely?

As Stern and Hammer (1978, p. 1105) observe, 'particular configurations of economic, political, and social factors have been present' in successful purchase negotiations between parent corporations and employee groups, 'and absent in the failures'. Various attempts have been made to identify the key ingredients in successful buyouts under different circumstances (Stern and Hammer, 1978; Bradley and Gelb, 1983a; Wright and Coyne, 1985). Three groups of characteristics have been stressed as important for success: (i) the buyers' desire, balance of skills, leadership and the ability to finance the purchase; (ii) the vendors' desire and agreement; and (iii) external factors, such as local trade union response, government, institutional and community support. The last category, including the increasing availability of finance and recent favourable changes in company law and taxation, may explain the dramatic growth in buyouts. However, a successful transfer of ownership is primarily contingent upon the buyer's desire and ability to finance a purchase. In this section the coincidence of interests between the vendor and the buyout consortium is examined, although the focus is primarily on the vendor. The next chapter looks more closely at the buyer's interests.

The different reasons for corporate divestment suggest that buyouts take place in many different contexts. Despite this heterogeneity, only one main theoretical approach has been developed to explain why buyouts take place, which we call the financial markets hypothesis. In this view, a buyout attempt is a function of an enterprise's inability to raise external equity capital (Bradley and Gelb, 1983a; Stern and Hammer, 1978). The lower the interest of the external investment community in a plant or firm no longer required by its owners, the greater may be the vendor's willingness to sell to a buyout consortium, and the latter's need to internalise equity capital and risk.

Firms in some circumstances may face this dilemma. The classic case is the company that must be closed (unless a buyer is found) because of trading losses, declining markets or management, or employee or trade union resistance to change. For the vendor, a buyout may preserve the corporate image, whilst yielding a higher net cash return than closure, even after a substantial discount on the sale price. For the buyout consortium, the purchase may be a long-term strategy to save a plant or firm. A similar situation may also occur in a moderately profitable enterprise which has suffered temporary setbacks or has been divested by a corporation that wishes to relocate capital for higher returns. As other corporate buyers may have similar expectations, a conventional external sale at a price close to asset value may not be possible. A buyout attempt may be a temporary arrangement to maintain the plant whilst the local capital market adjusts to the firm's changed circumstances.

The absence of other purchasers is not sufficient to ensure a successful buyout. Buyouts from plant shutdowns may be prevented by problems of financing, lack of local trade union support or other external factors. In addition, the vendors may be unwilling to sell to employees in some cases if (i) the new firm is likely to be a competitive threat, (ii) greater revenue can be realised from closure, or (iii) negotiations are likely to disclose confidential information.

The financial markets hypothesis needs to be understood in its context. Bradley and Gelb (1983a and 1985) developed their model from an investigation of a series of employee buyout conversions of plants facing closure in the late 1970s, when such buyouts were a relatively new phenomenon. Financial institutions were sceptical about financing plants facing closure which required high gearing. Finance therefore was available only from public sources or from those close to the firm.[6] But in recent years the financial markets have regarded employee buyout attempts more favourably. This shift is due to various changes in those markets, including deregulation; the increasing number of foreign banks who wish to find an entry into the British finance sector; and the increasing number of American banks with experience in highly leveraged deals, including Employee Stock Ownership Plants. Williams (1982) suggested that this may even be the main reason for the growth in buyouts.

As the buyout phenomenon widens to embrace more circumstances, the embryonic financial markets hypothesis developed by Bradley and Gelb

(1983a) has to be adapted to changed circumstances. For example, a significant number of employee buyouts have involved corporate divestments of potentially profitable units. Such buyouts may be completed even though rival external bids have been made (i.e. external capital seems willing to invest). In these cases the original financial markets hypothesis does not appear to hold. Such buyouts involve a distinctive kind of coincidence of interests between the purchaser and the seller. From the vendor's perspective, a protracted sale might attract management resistance, union opposition or difficult negotiations with an outside buyer. In particular managers of a potentially profitable enterprise may be prepared to become major risk-bearers in return for independence and the incentives of ownership. In instances where management is a potential buyer and an important element in a firm's assets, a vendor might accept a management buyout at a discount price because the alternative might be an even lower sale price in the event of the departure of key managers.

Early empirical evidence from North America and Britain provides mixed support for the financial markets hypothesis. (See for example, Zwerdling, 1978; Stern et al., 1979; Bradley and Gelb, 1983a.) In the 1970s, at least 100 buyouts took place in the United States, mostly in response to threatened plant closures. Like the North American buyouts, the 'Benn' cooperatives in Britain internalised capital in order to maintain the existence of a plant.[7] However, in the cases of the Scottish News Enterprises (Bradley and Gelb, 1983a) and Kirby Manufacturing and Engineering Company Ltd (Coates, 1976; Eccles, 1981) the commercial viability of the enterprises was dubious. Their relatively quick demise was in direct contrast to the experiences of North American buyouts.

Management buyouts in Britain appear to differ significantly from buyouts in the face of plant closure. Wright and Coyne (1985) revealed that 18 per cent of the management buyouts in their survey resulted from independent or parent companies in receivership. During the recession between 1979 and 1983, the unwillingness of capital to invest had been a major incentive for many managers to internalise capital. The vendors were willing to sell to management consortia in order to complete transactions quickly and cheaply. On the other hand, over 61 per cent of management buyouts resulted from corporate divestitutes of subsidiaries.[8] In many of these cases, capital was internalised to ensure economic survival, but most of the enterprises were relatively profitable. Indeed, these buyouts cannot be separated from the demerger boom or the new emphasis on the advantages of being small and independent. Therefore, the nature of the coincidence of interests between vendor and buyer is somewhat different.

17

The political economy of privatisation

The motivations for sales of nationalised enterprises are ideological and political as well as economic. The Conservative government of Margaret Thatcher believes that the public interest is best served by a wide dispersion of share ownership and by employees having an ownership stake in their own company. Moreover, sales of nationalised enterprises offer short-term revenue gains that permit the government greater flexibility in directing expenditures to high-priority areas or reducing taxes. In addition, several kinds of economic benefits might be expected from privatisation (although the empirical evidence is inconclusive). For example, privatised firms may be better able to avoid harmful ministerial interference, and the discipline of financial and product markets may motivate privatised firms to greater efficiency and effectiveness.

The debate about the benefits of privatisation has revolved around four main criteria: individual liberty; productive efficiency; public expenditure and fiscal policy; and the power of public sector unions. These four criteria can be interpreted to present three competing explanations for the privatisation programme since 1979: ideological, economic and political. Of the three, the political arguments are often the most convincing, but the phenomenon is perhaps best explained by a coincidence of all three explanatory approaches.

Liberty and nationalisation

The question of liberty generates strong ideological arguments both for and against privatisation. One of the main sources of division has to do with the relative importance of social freedom that can be fostered by the state, and individual liberty. In the early post-war period the balance of opinion appeared to have shifted towards state intervention. An important objective of early post-war nationalisation was to achieve the 'common ownership of the means of production, distribution and exchange', replacing private property and profits with ownership by the people: a socialist goal. Moreover, it was believed that the conflict between capital and labour would be reduced by the concentration of ownership in the state. Nationalisation was also seen as enabling economic planning. Economic freedom frequently failed to satisfy certain public needs, including economic stability, long-term investment and full employment. This failure had occasionally been acknowledged before 1945, notably during wartime when strategic industries came under public control. Nationalisation of 'the commanding heights of the economy' facilitated planning during peacetime to achieve those objectives. Furthermore, nationalised industries would be 'the high custodians of the public interest', fulfilling social and redistributive objectives (Morrison, 1933: p. 157).

Despite consensus on this issue in the early post-war years, libertarians since Hayek (1944) have been concerned about the dangers socialist collectivism and state planning pose to individual freedom, which they take to be the highest moral principle. Friedman (1962) saw economic intervention by the state as the greatest threat to liberty, since it concentrated economic and political power. The divorce between economic and political power implied by contracting the state's role was both necessary and sufficient for greater freedom. Joseph (1975), among others, challenged the notion that a minimal state role was sufficient to secure the greatest freedom.[9] Any high concentration of economic power, in his view, threatened freedom.

Joseph's (1975) view has implications both for the status of nationalised industries and for how they should be dismantled and reallocated. According to the Thatcher Conservative government, individual ownership of capital should be dispersed as widely as possible,[10] especially among employees, in order to create a 'people's capital market' (Moore, 1984).[11] Furthermore, in the Conservative government's view, the division between capital and labour can be mitigated by encouraging employees to participate in their company's financial arrangements, to foster an identification with capital (Green Paper, 1986). Nationalised industries, therefore, obstruct the breakdown of capital–labour distinctions, as 'only in nationalised concerns... are employees debarred from owning a stake in the business in which they spend their working lives' (Moore, 1983).

Privatisation has an overall ideological consistency in its objectives, namely to inaugurate a new era of free enterprise, political freedom and a 'property-owning democracy'. However, the issue of employee shareholding reveals an internal ideological tension between greater economic freedom, which implies the allocation of resources by market forces, and employee or people's share ownership which requires intervening in the market. The case for privatisation as a means of extending liberty is therefore primarily ideological, but its implementation may require priorities to be chosen. These choices are normative and any evaluation lies beyond the scope of this book.

The efficiency of nationalised industries

The case for privatising nationalised industries in order to improve their productive efficiency is primarily an economic argument for the transfer of ownership. The relevant theoretical and empirical literature is ambiguous, and suggests that any discussion of the relative merits of public and private ownership for productive efficiency should be confined to particular firms or sectors. Ownership may in some cases be less important for enterprise efficiency than factors such as industrial structure and the quality of management (Beesley and Littlechild, 1983).

The post-war Labour government expected productive efficiency to be improved by the nationalisation of 'the commanding heights of the economy'. In the case of natural monopolies, public ownership was viewed as the only way to realise the benefits of economies of scale without the abuse of monopoly power.[12] In industries where competition was possible, it was considered wasteful. Statutory monopolies eliminated the private shareholder, abolished the need to pay dividends and thereby lowered costs to the consumer. In addition, nationalisation was expected to generate economies of scale in certain industries which the free market could not achieve, and to internalise externalities to provide a more desirable overall outcome.[13] The nationalised industries were to be the fulcrum for reconstruction and economic growth in the post-war period.

Nationalisation may have been a response to market failures in the private sector, but it was not always clear why the public sector would do better (Perotin and Estrin, 1986). Factors obstructing market efficiency may have persisted under public ownership, but evaluation of the performance of nationalised industries is problematic. For monopoly industries there are no control groups, and non-monopoly public sector firms may be operating in very different market conditions to their private sector comparators. However, most observers have concluded that overall performance of the British nationalised sector has been disappointing (for example, Pryke, 1981; Redwood, 1980; Redwood and Hatch, 1982; Shackleton, 1984).[14] But empirical evidence on the relative performance of public and private enterprise is limited and ambivalent. Millward (1982) argues that private superiority has not been proven and that the importance of ownership has been exaggerated. Losses incurred by some nationalised enterprises may have been due to ministerial interventions, the primacy of social objectives or declining markets, and not necessarily due to poor cost efficiency. Yarrow (1986) summarised some of the international evidence on the comparative performance of public and private enterprises and found that although most of the studies favoured private enterprise, the evidence was far from overwhelming.[15]

An alternative empirical approach may be to assess the performance of firms before and after privatisation. As the pioneer, Britain has the most experience with privatisation. Although post-privatisation performance does seem to suggest some economic basis for preferring private ownership, there is also countervailing evidence. One of the most economically successful privatised companies is Associated British Ports. Before privatisation the docks were synonymous with strikes and inefficiency. After privatisation the company's progress was slow and uninspired, and it was hurt very badly by the 1984–5 miners' strike. However, since then, largely as a result of its property assets, it has performed exceedingly well. In February 1983, the date Associated British Ports was floated, issue price of its shares was 56p. The 1988 share price of some 565p represented about a 900 per cent increase.

Another significant economic success is the much larger Cable and Wireless, whose shares were issued at 56p in October 1981 and are now valued at around 344p, an increase in excess of 514 per cent. Other good performers include Amersham International, British Aerospace and Enterprise Oil. The more recent privatisations of TSB (November 1986), British Gas (December 1986), British Airways (February 1987), Rolls Royce (May 1987) and the British Airports Authority (July 1987) have not fared so well. However, as the programme did not really get under way until 1981, post-privatisation performances should be evaluated cautiously.

Given inconclusive empirical evidence, the case for privatisation has relied largely upon theory relating to four sources of potential inefficiency in nationalised industries. Firstly, it is argued that public sector monopolies abuse their market power. The failures of the natural monopolies in the public utilities were the outcome of public ownership rather than market failures (Sharkey, 1982). If an industry is a natural monopoly, it is desirable, by definition, that it be occupied by a single firm, provided it does not abuse its position by monopolistic behaviour.[16] Vickers and Yarrow (1985) identified four options for achieving this objective: (i) public ownership; (ii) competition, in the form of threat of entry; (iii) regulation, by agencies with power to monitor prices, output, etc., and (iv) franchising, that is, competition for the right to be the sole firm in an industry. They compared these possible options in telecommunications and electricity supply. Although each option had drawbacks, public ownership and regulated private ownership were found to be superior to the others.

In artificial statutory monopolies, increasing competition by the removal of controls on entry and licensing may improve the overall efficiency of the industry without regulation. Kay and Silberston (1984) argue that if the introduction of competition conflicts with a transfer of ownership, priority should be given to ensuring competition. However, competition without a transfer of ownership may be ineffective. The profit motive may quickly diminish in the public sector if profits are transferred elsewhere and losses remain subsidised.[17]

The second source of productive inefficiency is the institutional weakness of the relationship between nationalised industries and government. The Morrisonian public corporation model had intended to establish an arm's length relationship between government and the nationalised industries (Morrison, 1933). Post-war policies towards the industries were embodied in the statutes setting up the public corporations,[18] and in three White Papers which established guidelines to supplement the statutory duties, and increasingly demanded that nationalised industries perform like private firms (Treasury, 1961; 1967; 1978). However, the combination of vague objectives and persistent direct ministerial interventions into corporate decision-making, often for short-term political reasons, rendered these guidelines less effective. Monitoring management performance in the public sector is also a problem. In economies where a stock market can effectively monitor management performance in private firms, the advantages of public ownership may be outweighed by the costs of bureaucratic management due to the absence of profit-motivated shareholders.

Vickers and Yarrow (1985 and 1988) suggest that the problem is not immutable and that the productive efficiency of the nationalised industries could be improved by redefining the relationship between the industries and government. But the arguments against bureaucratic inefficiency and the political advantages of privatisation are forceful. Privatisation removes the institutional framework of public ownership, but it does not always preclude a high level of public control or influence. In some cases, short-term interventions to achieve tactical or social objectives can still be made either through the regulatory bodies or through shares in the privatised companies retained by the state.

Thirdly the nationalised industries' insulation from the financial markets provides a generally strong economic case for privatisation. Resources in the public sector are allocated through a political process, so that nationalised industries do not compete for finance in the same way that private firms do. This often creates a soft budget constraint which may foster inefficiency (Kornai, 1980). State-owned firms are not subject to the threat of bankruptcy, takeover or the disapprobation of shareholders. Of course very large private sector firms are also shielded from these pressures to some extent, because of the difficulties of takeovers and the likelihood of government intervention in the case of failure in a major British industry. The case appears strong though where small firms are concerned.[19]

Public sector finance has its own problems for some firms. The loan-based capital structure in most public enterprises may burden the industries with high interest repayments (Lumby, 1981). Financially sound enterprises may be able to handle debt, but others, possibly those in highly competitive markets, may have difficulty meeting deadweight interest repayments during poor performance periods when recapitalisation and investment are required. In these cases, the opportunity to enter the capital markets freely might be welcomed. Some nationalised industries have attempted to do so (Steel, 1984). For example, in 1982 British Telecommunications attempted to raise its own capital by a bond issue. Its failure strengthened the case for privatisation as the only way to restore capital efficiency (Brittan, 1984).

A similar argument applies to the fourth source of inefficiency in nationalised industries: insulation from product markets. The dynamic effects of the profit motive and competition, which generate quality of service, innovation and consumer sovereignty, are generally absent. Nationalised industries are often prevented by statue from diversifying. Moreover, political pressure locks them into activities from which, on a purely commercial basis, they ought to withdraw. Behaviour becomes dysfunctional, and their financial position steadily declines.

Despite some obvious failings in the nationalised industries, a simple transfer of ownership need not lead to immediate and clear changes. Furthermore, reform may be possible within the public sector. For example, the relationship between government and industry might be improved; or it might be possible to relax entry conditions, allow direct access to capital, introduce regulatory bodies to control pricing, output, investment, etc., and change managerial incentives and controls. These options have not been carefully considered on a case-specific basis. Nevertheless, the most convincing economic case for privatisation of state industries remains the expected benefits to productive efficiency. We now turn to the third major issue in the privatisation debate: public expenditure and fiscal strategy.

Public expenditure and fiscal strategy

The consequences of privatisation for public expenditure are uncertain. There is some agreement about the need to control public expenditure and to invest in more productive sectors (see, for example, Bacon and Eltis, 1978), but the implications of sales for monetary growth are unclear. Clearly, however, one of the strongest political cases for privatisation of state enterprises is that it enables a more flexible fiscal strategy. Acute budgetary pressures create difficulties for orthodox politico-economic management. The financing of growing budget deficits by conventional Keynesian methods (i.e. through increased taxation or increased borrowing) are challenged by political considerations or by monetarism. Therefore, asset sales will often further the pursuit of short-term political objectives.

In the British case, the economic effects of privatisation on public expenditure were of significance to the Conservative government immediately after its election victory in 1979. The first Expenditure Plans stated the government's belief that 'public expenditure is at the heart of Britain's economic difficulties' (Treasury, 1980). In 1979 the net deficits of public corporations totalled 5 per cent of public expenditure. As part of the new programme 'special asset sales' were used to reduce the Public Sector Borrowing Requirement (PSBR) (Howe, 1981; Treasury, 1980; 1981). Receipts from sales were used by the Exchequer as revenue, and the nationalised industries' borrowing was reduced or eliminated. Moreover, hybrid organisations' borrowings were also removed from the PSBR figures.[20]

There is a difference between the long- and short-run net effects of sales on revenue to the Exchequer. In the short run, there are revenue gains. During 1979–84, the sale of public enterprises and council housing reduced the PSBR annually by 20 to 30 per cent (Pauley, 1984). This facilitated a reduction in the rate of monetary growth in each of those years. However, the long-run consequences of asset sales, notably on interest rates, are less clear. Peacock and Shaw (1981) convincingly argue that privatised concerns may place an upward pressure on interest rates as they seek investible funds in the private sector. A government's loss of receipts from profitable industries may not be recovered in tax revenue. If taxes are not increased, this will put an additional upward pressure on interest rates. On the other hand, asset sales reduce the need for gilt sales, so that less needs to be spent on future debt and interest repayments. The conclusion reached is that reliable predictions about the long-term effects of privatisation on the PSBR are not possible.[21]

However privatisation affects long-term monetary growth, it offers the obvious short-term political advantage of immediate revenue gains. Increased fiscal flexibility enables either a reduction in taxation, or a reduction in the pressures upon public expenditure programmes. From 1979 onwards, several factors made the Conservative government's attempt to control and reduce public expenditure problematic. Firstly, the government had its own political spending priorities, namely defence, and law and order.[22] Secondly, political opposition inhibited the government from cutting expenditure on other programmes. The desire of ministers, civil servants and pressure groups to protect their interests may produce additional resistance within the government. Thirdly, a combination of demographic and economic factors has dramatically increased expenditure on demand-related services, for example in health, education and social security.[23] With more people subsisting on social security, benefit-erosion has become politically more difficult. Privatisation of state industries may be a way of increasing fiscal flexibility in order to achieve short-term political advantage.

Public sector trade unions

Restraining trade union power may be a final motivation for privatising state industries. There are strong economic and political arguments for doing so. Economic arguments are based on the advantages to be gained from exposing trade to the pressures of market forces in the private sector. The political case is that privatisation is a way for government to divest responsibility for public sector unions. The burden of responsibility is transferred out of the public domain, reducing the temptation to intervene in disputes and the electorate's expectations that government will do so. Interventions may nevertheless still be made for social, economic or political reasons.

The economic case rests on two assumptions:
(i)   that the subordination of the labour market institutions to those of the product and financial markets is desirable and is best achieved by exposure to market forces;
(ii) that privatisation actually achieves that objective.

A major aim of nationalisation was to improve industrial relations. Trade union recognition and collective bargaining procedural arrangements embodied in the nationalisation statutes were intended to establish a framework within which to improve industrial relations and increase worker influence (Crosland, 1956). The Donovan Commission (1968) supported these objectives. It characterised the main British industrial relations problem as a lack of formal institutions and procedures for negotiation and consultation in the private manufacturing sector, which led to wages drift and unofficial industrial action. At the same time the relatively centralised and institutionalised public sector was comparatively stable.[24] The implication was that the institutions for industrial relations regulation may actually improve industrial relations and performance.

Economists have tended to focus upon the anti-competitive or monopoly effects of trade unionism. In a study of union and non-union firms in the United States' private sector, Freeman and Medoff (1984) developed an alternative approach. They suggested that unions on balance played a beneficial role in improving workplaces, facilitating the functioning of internal labour markets, and increasing productivity; the monopoly power of trade unions was outweighed by the benefits from their voice-response function.[25]

The steady post-war growth of public expenditure up to the mid-1970s provided a sheltered bargaining context. Comparability was an accepted guiding principle for fixing wage claims, and the extensive arbitration machinery supported settlements by peaceful means (Winchester, 1983). Public sector trade unions often had great bargaining strength. Drawing on the so-called bottomless pit of the public purse, governments were often willing to underwrite large wage claims and overmanning. By the 1970s the situation was changing dramatically, as the restraint of public expenditure became viewed as a way of controlling inflation.[26] Numerous incomes policies from 1972 to 1979 distorted relativities and comparability in the public sector, resulting in several major official strikes, which tended to be longer and more tightly organised than those in the private sector. A Conservative Party study group concluded that trade unions were so strong in certain nationalised industries that, 'where they have the nation by the jugular vein, the only option is to pay up'.[27]

Exposure to the greater pressure of market forces in the private sector was felt to be one way of generating greater responsibility in public sector trade unions. Tipping the balance of power towards management in the industries concerned would encourage a restructuring of industrial relations and improvements in productive efficiency.[28]

Empirical evidence of the effects of privatisation on the trade unions is limited and ambiguous. The change in ownership often removes the statutory protection of trade union recognition and collective bargaining rights. As a result these rights are apparently being eroded in some of the weaker sectors of those enterprises which were fragmented after privatisation, such as British Transport Hotels (Trades Union Congress, 1986). However, this experience has not been universal. On substantive issues, trade union power has not necessarily diminished. Vickers and Yarrow (1985) observe that the power of trade unions at Jaguar increased after privatisation. Moreover, if natural monopolies remain structurally similar after a transfer of ownership to the private sector, privatisation will not necessarily weaken trade union bargaining strength, as wage claims can be passed to the consumer relatively easily in the form of higher prices or lower output. We attempt to shed more light on this issue with evidence from the NFC.

The political case for weakening public sector unions is largely self-evident. Conservative governments are generally happy to undermine the power of monopoly trade unions. They transfer to the private sector the burden of responsibility for controlling those trade unions, as well as responsibility for the social costs which slow the processes of contraction and reconstruction in declining industries. An important part of this effort has been the generous employee shareholding arrangements accompanying most major privatisations. These schemes aim both to overcome employees' resistance to changes in ownership and in their terms and conditions of employment, and to undermine union opposition to privatisation.

Summary

The case for the privatisation of state industries has several strands. The argument that privatisation is a prerequisite for increasing individual liberty is largely an ideological one, not open to empirical investigation. There is an economic basis for other arguments, namely the inefficiencies of nationalised industries, the lack of control over natural monopolies, and the need to restrain public expenditure and public sector unions. Although a strong case can be made for privatising some public enterprises for these reasons, benefits may not be applicable to every firm. Clearly, however, privatisation has distinct advantages as a political strategy, because of budgetary strains, public sector monopoly trade union power and the unpopularity of nationalised industries. The phenomenon is perhaps best explained by a coincidence of the ideological, economic and political motives.

Public sector buyouts

Why does the privatisation of some state industries result in sales to employee or management consortia? We approach this question by suggesting situations in which the potential for a buyout exists and then evaluating the costs and benefits of a possible buyout to the primary groups concerned, and in particular a government and a buyout consortium. Unorthodox strategies may be sought for the sale of certain enterprises to be privatised. A buyout therefore may be a pragmatic response representing the best feasible option.[29] The first step, however, is to examine the nature of public enterprises in Britain, and to assess the early financial markets hypothesis developed above.

Public enterprises and methods of disposal

Crosland (1956) argued that the broad objectives of public ownership pointed towards nationalisation of certain industries. However, this defence of the nationalised sector appears to some extent to have been an *ex-post* rationalisation of the Labour government's programme between 1945 and 1951. Indeed, there appears to have been a general lack of consistency in nationalisation policy. In the initial post-war phase, some enterprises were taken over for essentially ideological and political reasons, such as the coal and steel industries. But other sectors in which nationalisation could have been recommended for similar reasons (for example, the commercial banking system, which is nationalised in some countries) remained untouched. The illogicalities continued in the 1950s. The Labour government renationalised steel after it had been denationalised, but not the bulk of road haulage, which had been denationalised between 1953 and 1956.[30] During 1970–4, the Heath Conservative government took both Rolls Royce and British Leyland into public ownership. Indeed, 'there is no coherent defence of the overall size and composition of this sector...' (Shackleton, 1984, p. 62).

By 1979, the public sector included a diverse collection of commercial and non-commercial activities. Commercial activities differed considerably in their success and profitability. The most desirable, and therefore the easiest to sell in the conventional financial markets, were: (i) natural monopolies; (ii) cash-rich, efficient and independent organisations; (iii) portfolio investments in major British companies; (iv) efficient and profitable subsidiaries of the public corporations.

Less desirable were basically profitable enterprises which needed cash injections, new management, rationalisation, debt cancellation, or pensions deficiency payments. This category, which included the essentially profitable subsidiaries of public corporations whose profits were being used for cross-subsidisation, were reasonably easy to sell in favourable market conditions, however. Least desirable were a rump of poorly performing enterprises in declining sectors, with strong trade unions likely to resist rationalisation. In these cases, the financial markets would have functioned efficiently only if the sales were at very large discounts on asset value.

Given this range of desirability, most sales will involve the relatively attractive enterprises. But the determination of government ministers may override the difficulties of selling less desirable enterprises. Marketability may then influence the method of sale employed, rather than the decision whether to sell at all.

Figure 2.1 shows the different ways of transferring ownership to the private sector. Two main methods of sale are available for blue chip enterprises: (i) public flotation, and (ii) direct sale to a third party. Public flotations can take two forms: (a) a fixed price offer for sale in the Stock Exchange, in which anybody who wishes to buy shares at the fixed price may do so. The number of shares sold to applicants may well be scaled down in the event of an oversubscription; and (b) an offer for sale by tender on the Stock Exchange, in which a striking price is announced and

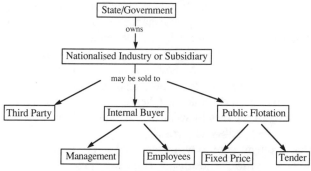

Figure 2.1 Methods of sale in privatisation

anybody who tenders at that price or above receives shares. Public flotation in either of these ways is best suited to larger companies; the assumption is that the financial markets will respond favourably to the offer to secure a satisfactory price for the sale (Coyne and Wright, 1982a; Pickering, 1984).

A direct sale to a third party may be more appropriate for companies too small to float. This approach can also be used in cases where the financial markets may not respond at a satisfactory price, but the integration of the buyers' and the privatised concerns' activities may generate benefits to the owners, the consumer and a government. In these situations bidders can either tender or conduct lengthier negotiations to complete a sale.

Although an employee or management buyout represents a less desirable method of sale, such arrangements are not confined to the least desirable of state-owned enterprises. Indeed, buyouts are more likely to occur in basically viable businesses whose marketability has been affected by short-term performance forecasts or whose return on investment is too low to attract corporate investors.

This financial markets hypothesis cannot explain the encouragement of employee ownership for non-market reasons, a factor that is much more likely to be important in the public sector than in the private sector. Like privatisation itself, the development of share ownership schemes for employees seems to be explained by a combination of ideological, political and economic factors. We have already argued that one of the government's ideological objectives in privatisation has been to create a property-owning democracy as a counter to socialism. Sales have been accompanied by cheap offers of shares to employees, with the goal of increasing their identification with capital. From an economic perspective, shares for employees can be seen as an attempt to harmonise industrial relations perhaps leading to improved company performance. This point is related to the political explanation for share schemes. A major objective of privatisation is to improve cost-efficiency which may involve putting new pressures on employees' productivity. Demands for increased competitiveness and profitability in the private sector may also squeeze wages and conditions, and weaken the trade unions. Cheap share offers may be viewed as an incentive to employees to swallow this bitter pill, or at least to avert outright employee hostility to the sale.

The employee share schemes embody a fundamental contradiction or internal tension in privatisation: subsidising employee share ownership clearly conflicts with the major objective of allocating resources by market forces.[31] Single-minded pursuit of market efficiency would prohibit this approach to creating a property-owning democracy. The employee buyout route to privatisation may present similar dilemmas for policy-makers. Nevertheless, if privatisation is to be extended beyond the sale of the blue chip enterprises, priorities have to be chosen. We will attempt to incorporate this point into an application of the financial markets approach to buyouts from the public sector.

Financial markets hypothesis

Government

By government we mean the cabinet, including the minister of the sponsoring department, and assume that all parties within the government have identical interests: to achieve successful and complete sales. Consequently the desirable industries will be the most likely to be sold. The need for short-term revenue to achieve a more flexible fiscal policy may also accelerate the sale of blue chip enterprises. However, privatisation may produce some of its great benefits – in improving competition, enhancing the company's efficiency, reducing public expenditure and the power of monopoly trade unions – when less desirable enterprises are divested. One method of doing so may be a buyout.

In the sale of certain concerns marketability is not wholly a financial problem. The reluctance of outside private capital to enter a troubled industry, temporarily or otherwise, could usually be overcome by sufficiently lowering the sale price. However, if a large discount is required to complete a sale, a government may have to consider other factors. Any cheap offers in the conventional financial markets may attract aggressive domestic bidders who would strip the company's assets and create redundancies, or foreign buyers, either of which may be considered unacceptable. A government determined to sell, even at a discount, may prefer to transfer ownership to a management or employee consortium rather than to any other investor. For buyouts too, experience in the private sector indicates a discount may be required to achieve a successful sale.

An employee buyout offers several advantages to a government attempting to dispose of an enterprise. Firstly, it can extend privatisation into declining industries, such as parts of coal-mining, steel manufacturing and shipbuilding, which have losses or low returns and long-run marketability problems. In these cases, competition from substitute products or foreign trade has steadily and irrevocably reduced the demand for, and volume of, production of a particular product. As the British economy has adjusted to these changes, the external costs, often cited as the reasons for nationalisation and subsidisation, have gradually diminished. In some cases, external costs may now be confined to local economies and the employees of the establishments concerned.

Given these circumstances, a government may be more willing to consider reducing or even ending subsidisation, by contracting, closing or divesting an enterprise. Divestment is virtually impossible for some enterprises; as the demand for these industries continues to erode, the only feasible options are likely to be closure, contraction or continuing subsidisation. Examples include shipbuilding, coal-mining, some steel plants and volume car production. Greater potential exists: (i) in profitable establishments or niches within declining industries which are profitable; (ii) where the potential for profits on a small scale may exist; or, (iii) in cases where closures and contraction may prove costly.

A government may, therefore, be willing to consider divesting certain enterprises by discounted employee buyouts. Such a course can ease the costs of decline in a productive way while ending a longer-term commitment. Moreover, as discussed in the third set of hypotheses below, the incentives of community and employee ownership may improve the efficiency of the enterprises concerned, generating some of the greatest economic and political benefits from privatisation.

A government may also consider an employee buyout option if an enterprise to be sold is essentially profitable, but cannot be sold immediately, at an acceptable price to outside buyers with acceptable aspirations, because of temporary setbacks due to restructuring or a lapse in demand. A buyout may also enable a government to sell an enterprise in its entirety rather than sell it off piecemeal. If the enterprise is dismantled, its less desirable components, which may have been preventing a conventional sale in the first place, may prove difficult to dispose of. Additionally, the fragmentation of an organisation may lead to the loss of head office and other jobs when the separated units are integrated into other organisations. If a buyout bid is made to keep the organisation together, it may deter other potential bidders who would be unwilling to cope with a management which gives no warranties to the buyer and which may subsequently be obstructive. Thus the very existence of a buyout bid may propel a government towards having to accept it.

The political benefits from privatisation by employee buyouts have no parallel in the private sector. A buyout may also deflect the criticism that privatisation amounts to selling off some of the nation's most valuable assets, which were owned by the people (Manwaring and Sigler, 1985; Labour Research Department, 1985).[32] Pliatzky (1985) suggests that 'public ownership is not strictly ownership by the people' as the individual owner has no right to disposal. Nevertheless, this is primarily an ideological discussion about the relative merits of common and individual ownership. A buyout may be viewed as a third way between public and conventional private ownership which may make privatisation of state industries more acceptable. Similarly, because they extend share ownership to employees on a far larger scale, buyouts may be preferred to attempts to widen share ownership in the course of privatisation by offering discounted shares to employees and small investors.

Various obstacles may prevent a government from selling to a buyout consortium. As already mentioned, buyouts would not be easy in loss-making areas. They may also be unlikely in large, complex, capital-intensive organisations whose employees could not raise sufficient capital to finance the purchase. A higher offer made by an independent bidder would be difficult to refuse, even if management objected. In addition, although changes in taxation and company law since 1979 facilitate such sales, banks may be unwilling to finance a highly geared option when a more conventional solution is feasible. Other interests, considered below, may also resist. And the situation is different if an enterprise for sale has some private shareholders, even if government is the largest shareholder. It may no longer be possible to offer a discounted sale price to secure a sale, as this course might be against the interests of the private shareholders. The buyout option may therefore be more likely when share capital is fully in state or public ownership.

The Civil Service: Treasury and sponsoring department

The British Civil Service is traditionally neutral to the extent that senior officials do not change with governments. This neutrality has been reinforced by a division in functions between administration and policy-making; politicians make policy decisions while the Civil Service executes them. However, senior civil servants are continuously concerned with policy, and because the Civil Service is permanent, it has developed its own experience and expertise in formulating policy as well as its own vested interests. In addition, functional differentiation within the Civil Service has led to divisional interests. Thus the Civil Service cannot be regarded as void of vested interests.

Several departments within the Civil Service may be involved in the design and implementation of any privatisation programme. The main participants will be the Treasury, the sponsoring departments, the Department of Trade and Industry (when not itself a sponsoring department), the Bank of England and various policy units.

Tension may emerge between the Treasury and a sponsoring department, and between the policy and finance divisions of a given department. The main concern of the Treasury and finance divisions will be to ensure the financial propriety of any sale. In particular, the Treasury will attempt to protect the interests of the taxpayers. The sponsoring departments and policy divisions may be more concerned with issues such as the implications of a specific privatisation for employment levels, the quality of goods and services, and the customer and supplier responses to the restructuring. Differences need not be overt and may not break out in a dispute, but remain a potential source of tension.

Tensions are most likely to emerge on two core issues. Firstly, if the sale of the enterprise requires an enabling law before privatisation, when should it be incorporated? The Treasury may well favour late incorporation, since an earlier move might allow the industry concerned to escape the financial controls imposed by the government on the nationalised industries. On the other hand, sponsoring departments may prefer an early incorporation to allow the company time to establish itself before a flotation or sale.

The second source of tension may be the timing of the sale and the sale price. These two issues are closely related as the timing may well be determined by the enterprise's marketability. The Treasury will presumably emphasise securing as high a sale price as possible, while the sponsoring department may be more concerned with achievement of a smooth transfer, or the related policies on regulation and competition, and so on. Also, the Bank of England, with knowledge of other scheduled flotations that might strain the capital market's ability to respond, may offer advice on timing.

Conceivably unforeseen events might affect the marketability of an enterprise and prevent a conventional sale. Rather than wait for more favourable conditions, the Treasury and the sponsoring departments may prefer an alternative option, such as a buyout.

The enterprise for sale or its parents

The cooperation of the industry concerned is usually necessary for a smooth transfer of ownership from the public to the private sector. Little persuasion may be required for industries on the periphery of the public sector that operate mainly in highly competitive private sector markets. Alternatively, government has at least two ways to persuade public sector companies to cooperate: by appointing senior management favourable to privatisation, and by imposing tight fiscal controls. The latter approach may encourage the enterprise to seek private capital to finance growth and expansion. Major nationalised industries may also be encouraged to sell their peripheral activities to raise revenue.

We have not yet explained why any sale of a nationalised industry should result in a buyout, or should be encouraged by senior management. Indeed, if an organisation is facing cash flow difficulties, the highest sale price will be desired, which may prevent the discount necessary for a buyout. But in some instances the company may favour the buyout option. For example, a quick sale may be needed to relieve short-term cash flow problems or reassure customers and suppliers about the status of the company and its continued viability. Sometimes the only alternative to a discounted sale to a buyout consortium may be closure, which would involve high liquidation expenses, redundancy payments and possible disruptions. An employee buyout may seem preferable. Finally, a public corporation may wish to retain a subsidiary as a supplier or buyer. Coase (1937) argued that an activity should be conducted within the firm only if the costs of internal administration are less than the costs of market transactions. Nationalised industries may contain units which could successfully become independent whilst continuing to provide goods and services to the remaining company. A management or employee buyout may be the most feasible way of preventing the newly independent unit from seeking alternative contractual arrangements, particularly if it relies on the skills of the existing management or workforce.

The buyout consortium

In any privatisation of a state enterprise employees and managers may have both defensive and offensive objectives. A defensive objective will be to protect salaries, work conditions and job security. Sale of non-profitable units, or those with poor short-term marketability, may lead to job losses if plants are closed, the organisation is dismantled (undermining the jobs of central management and administrative staff) or the buyer plans to run down operations and sell the assets. After a sale the new owners may try to reduce production costs, putting new pressure on wages and conditions. The trade union and collective bargaining procedures may be weakened, and index-linked pensions discontinued. Another fear may be that relationships with customers and suppliers will be hurt by an announcement that a firm is for sale. Either to prevent sales to undesirable owners or to retain relationships with customers and suppliers, employees and/or management may consider making a defensive buyout bid.

More positive motivations may also be at work. The buyout consortium may stand to realise substantial capital gains, particularly if a conventional sale has been prevented only by a temporary marketability problem. The opportunities may be even greater if a discount can be negotiated on the sale price. If the gains are risky, few outside investors may be interested; and if the riskiness is reduced by retaining the expertise and commitment of the incumbent management or workforce, a buyout may be a highly attractive proposition (Coyne and Wright, 1982a). There will also be a momentum to distribute shares as widely as possible: (i) if it is difficult to raise the initial equity finance by a small group to secure a substantial internal control; (ii) to pool risks; and (iii) to reduce risks by ensuring that commitment and incentives are spread widely in the company, and to harmonise industrial relations.

To summarise, some nationalised businesses prove much easier to sell than others, through either a public flotation or a private sale. The buyout route may be chosen when a sale through the financial markets would require a heavily discounted price. This might be the case for a company in a declining industry or one that looks unattractive because of temporary setbacks in short-term performance. Selling a nationalised firm to its employees may also be a more politically defensible course than a conventional sale. From the perspective of employees and managers, a buyout may make it possible to avoid unwanted changes in the operation of the business and, if the sale price reflects a substantial discount, may offer the prospect of significant capital gains. The question of the buyout consortium's interests is closely linked to the employee investment decision, which is examined in Chapters 4 and 5.

3

Privatisation and employee ownership: the NFC conversion

Introduction

This chapter considers the case for privatising the National Freight Corporation which was formed in 1968 and which the Conservative government inherited in 1979. As the ideological argument is similar to that for any other nationalised industry, the analysis focuses on the economic and political cases. Overall, the performance history of the National Freight Corporation (NFC) and its predecessors in public sector road freight transport created considerable economic motivation: productive efficiency had been constrained under public ownership, and the potential existed for considerable efficiency gains from privatisation. But the inherited economic problems of the NFC made it a problematic case for conventional privatisation and therefore a candidate for an alternative solution.

The political case for privatising the NFC is less convincing. Revenue gains from selling the NFC would have been relatively small, and the enterprise was not unpopular with the electorate as it mainly serviced industry. Nor would the significant political gains be realised by removing the trade unions at the NFC from the public sector. In general, having needed relatively little public support, public sector road haulage activities have stayed out of the political limelight.

Origins of the NFC: the failure of integration

Between 1948 and 1979, the commercial efficiency of public sector road freight transport activities was subordinated to external political commitments for lengthy periods.[1] This politicisation hurt productive efficiency. The period from 1948 to 1970 was dominated by the shibboleth of transport integration, with the needs of public sector road freight subordinated to those of the railways. Road freight transport in 1948 was neither a natural monopoly nor part of the 'commanding heights of the economy'.

36

Nationalisation of the industry had more to do with the relationship to the railways than the need for centralised state ownership and control. Although transport integration failed, progress was made towards providing an integrated road haulage network. This had the disadvantage of mixing profitable units with inefficient ones. After 1970 the NFC attempted to modernise, but regulation of its capital requirements, and political constraints on product development and the organisation of labour, frustrated its efforts and made the enterprise difficult to sell at the time of privatisation.

Structure

Road freight transport activities were first nationalised in the Transport Act 1947. During the Second World War the state had controlled road transport through the Road Haulage Organisation. Close collaboration with the railways had provided temporarily an integrated network. The post-war Labour government intended to continue and improve the integration of road and rail transport as nationalised industries.

Indeed, 'nationalisation of transport was the most ambitious effort of the Labour Government of 1945' (Kelf-Cohen, 1973: p. 67). The Transport Act 1947 set up the British Transport Commission (BTC) which was to coordinate the development of a nationally integrated transport network. All land transport was controlled by the BTC through four Executives.[2] The Road Haulage Executive (RHE) was responsible for road haulage activities, and traded as British Road Services (BRS).

The Trades Union Congress (TUC) favoured nationalisation of the entire road transport network which had been controlled by the Road Haulage Organisation during the war. But it was difficult to nationalise such a fragmented industry. In the eventual policy nationalisation was confined to long distance hauliers.[3] Private hauliers were limited to a radius of 25 miles.[4] At the end of 1951, when the final takeovers were completed (despite resistance from some owners), BRS had acquired over 3,700 firms, owned some 41,000 vehicles, based upon 1,000 depots, and employed over 75,000 people. BRS' monopoly was consolidated by the BTC's control over the issuing of new licences to competitors.

The Road Haulage Executive faced one major organisational problem in implementing nationalisation in 1947. The fragmented and competitive nature of the industry meant that there was no established superstructure of head office and administration to coordinate the new national network. Indeed, because most of the acquired hauliers were small, there was often no local clerical staff; in many cases acquisition left the RHE with the vehicles, but no traffic, drivers or depots.

Once nationalisation was achieved (an accomplishment in itself) the problems of integration came to the fore. Plans presented by the British Transport Commission proved to be too ambitious.[5] As the NFC annual report for 1969 observed, 'A primary difficulty was that "integration" has never been clearly defined.' Completion of the programme was expected to take at least ten years. Given the lack of political consensus on the need for integration, a ten-year programme was unlikely to succeed. In addition, there were internal problems. Firstly, customers had a free choice between services provided within the nationalised sector, which encouraged competition rather than integration between various transport modes. Secondly, as private firms carrying their own goods were excluded from nationalisation, a large part of the industry stayed outside the public domain; firms using external hauliers were encouraged to set up in-house fleets.

'It is not surprising, therefore, that the advent of a Conservative government late in 1951 put an end to the various schemes of integration on which the Commission had laboured. For it was apparent that the Transport Commission was making slow progress in the great programme of integrating all forms of transport envisaged in the 1947 Act' (Kelf-Cohen, 1973: p. 75). The Transport Bill 1952 recommended denationalisation of most of the BTC's road haulage activities, but the eventual outcome was less extensive. The BTC's licence-issuing role was lifted, as was the 25-mile limit imposed on private hauliers. However, it proved impossible to reduce the number of vehicles to 2,300, as planned.[6] Furthermore, the government finally accepted that a state haulage fleet would provide a strategic advantage by augmenting the army's road transport. The BTC was therefore allowed to retain its trunk service which included some 8,000 vehicles.

The Transport Act 1956 signalled the end of denationalisation. Although the goal of transport integration was set aside, BRS remained larger than intended and larger than any private firm. It controlled 1 per cent of all goods vehicles in its weight classes, and 5 per cent of all hire and reward vehicles. Even so, for the first time, BRS was in direct competition with private hauliers. Moreover, as no full-scale renationalisation was ever attempted, state-owned freight interests have had to operate in domestic markets in which they did not have a monopoly or even a dominant position.

Initially, denationalisation hurt BRS' productive efficiency, in part because the composition of activities changed. The bulk of general haulage was sold in 1954, but the highly labour-intensive parcels-carrying sections remained. Moreover, denationalisation often resulted in just the sale of vehicles. There was no compulsion for buyers to take employees. The best

BRS management went into the private sector, but lower management, clerical and driving grades remained highly overmanned. Finally, the Conservative government switched investments in transport to the railways. For example, in 1956 a £90 million railways modernisation programme resulted in a £9 million reduction in BRS' capital expenditure. Without investment in new depots and vehicles, productivity suffered.

Although transport integration had been dropped, the BTC was still felt to be too railway-orientated. In 1960 a White Paper considered the need to decentralise all public sector transport activities.[7] The Transport Act 1962 dismantled the British Transport Commission (BTC), separated its various transport functions and passed all its road transport functions to a newly formed Transport Holding Company (THC).[8] The organisational structure of the new holding company decentralised operational responsibility to the individual companies. The monolithic and centralised structure set up in 1947 under the BTC was now completely demolished. However, the most important innovation in the Act was that the Transport Holding Company was instructed to operate as a commercial enterprise. The government suggested that BRS should not even be thought of as a nationalised industry as it was small, had a commercial structure and operated in competitive markets. Since 1956 BRS had had to generate business in fair competition with private hauliers in competitive product markets, and its performance had been steadily improving. The Transport Act 1962 consolidated this policy.

The 1962 Act also enabled the Transport Holding Company to grow by negotiating acquisitions in line with the general growth of road freight activity. This programme was accelerated after the return of a Labour government in 1964. A spate of takeovers were negotiated, though far more selectively than in the 1940s, in what became known as backdoor nationalisation. The number of vehicles increased by over 3,000 during 1964–6. By 1968, gross revenues for the entire BRS network reached the record level of £49.5 million.

The Transport Act 1968 represented the second and final attempt to integrate the freight transport sector after the Second World War. The Labour government's policy had unfolded in a series of papers during 1966–8. In 1967 a White Paper restated its commitment to integrate freight transport: 'Road and rail services which perform the same function must be integrated to improve their efficiency, and those which should be complementary must operate in a framework which encourages coordination' *(The Transport of Freight*, 1967). The White Paper (1967) recommended the formation of a National Freight Corporation to incorporate all road freight activities. Its role would be to set the framework within which the subsidiaries would operate, rather than to manage them.

Renewed attempt at integration

The Transport Act 1968 enacted the White Paper's (1967) recommendations. The new National Freight Corporation (NFC) integrated the various nationalised road freight transport activities, including activities previously undertaken by the British Railways Board (BRB).[9] The NFC was also given a 51 per cent holding in another BRB operation, Freightliners, whilst BRB retained the remaining 49 per cent which blurred the distinction between road and rail. The NFC's initial total capital was some £100 million, with an annual turnover of £170 million and 66,000 employees. In addition, the Act set up a Freight Integration Council to co-ordinate the distribution of freight by road and rail services throughout Britain.

The NFC represented a notable departure from previous attempts at integration. Within the NFC traffic was to be allocated purely on the basis of competition. Furthermore, commercial efficiency and competitiveness were important priorities. The NFC was to be 'non-monopolistic, non-bureaucratic and non-subsidised'. The Transport Act 1968, therefore, contained a basic contradiction: it reinforced the commercial nature of road haulage as laid down in the Transport Act 1962, whilst reviving regulation to achieve integration.

After 1968, political commitments impaired the NFC's early commercial efficiency. Initially the main problem was that the 1968 Act had specified that as much freight as possible should go by rail when it was economic and efficient to do so.[10] It was difficult to prove that railways were more economic and efficient, and the policy was never implemented. The necessary regulations were not formulated before the departure of the Labour government in June 1970, and the return of a Conservative government signalled the end to integration.

Profitability

The evidence relating to BRS' productive efficiency and profitability between 1948 and 1968 is conflicting.[11] Performance indicators compare favourably with other nationalised industries, but not with the private road freight sector. However, comparisons with the private sector are suspect. To begin with, most private hauliers were restricted to journeys of 25 miles or less during the monopoly situation. Moreover, the fragmented nature of the industry has made it difficult to compile industry statistics; available figures tend to be unreliable.

BRS made profits in every year between 1948 and 1968, excluding 1950. As a percentage of net assets BRS' profits were higher than in the rest of the nationalised sector during the same period, although generally somewhat lower than in the private manufacturing sector. Pryke (1971)

Table 3.1. *Freight transport in Great Britain: 1954 and 1974* (,000 mill. ton-km)

Mode of transport	1954	%	1974	%
Road	34.5	37.4	89.9	65.1
Rail	36.1	39.2	24.2	17.5
Coastal shipping	21.1	22.9	20.5	14.8
Pipeline	0.2	0.2	3.4	2.5
Inland waterways	0.3	0.3	0.1	0.1
All freight transport	92.2	100.0	138.1	100.0
Licensed haulage vehicles (,000)	1,097		1,778	

Source: *Transport Policy: A Consultation Document*, HMSO, London, 1976.

showed that the performance of the nationalised sector from 1948 to 1968 fell into two distinct periods, and the same can be said of BRS.[12] For example, between 1948 and 1968 BRS' labour productivity increased at an average of 3.1 per cent per annum, but the rate was less than 1 per cent during the 1948–58 period and almost 5 per cent between 1958 and 1968. These figures were below the nationalised sector's average, but compared favourably with the private manufacturing sector, particularly between 1958 and 1968. Finally, between 1958 and 1968, BRS' output per man hour improved by 62 per cent which was above the public sector average for that period.

Overall, BRS' performance appears to be good, but there was considerable variation between sectors; general haulage and parcels were less successful. Indeed, 'developments in the haulage field continue to underline the wisdom of the Group companies in concentrating on specialist traffics and on contract hire'.[13] Moreover, BRS' performance should be viewed in the light of the rapid post-war increase in the demand for road freight transport. Between 1954 and 1974 the volume of road freight nearly trebled, while its share of the total freight doubled to over 65 per cent (Table 3.1). Mechanisation and containerisation account for the relatively smaller growth in the number of licensed haulage vehicles; these trends also boosted productivity, as did changing speed limits.

Comparisons of the relative profitability of public and private sector hauliers would be illuminating, but few such studies exist. One source is the Road Haulage Association's evidence to the Prices and Incomes Board in 1967.[14] A comparison was made of profit as a percentage of turnover in BRS and ten private companies between 1963 and 1967. All the private companies were medium-sized, although the industry includes many small

Table 3.2. *Profit as a percentage of turnover: BRS and ten private companies compared*

	1963	1964	1965	1966	1967
Private companies	9.8	9.8	10.5	9.0	4.2
All BRS	7.5	10.3	8.8	5.5	3.3
BRS General*	3.5	7.4	6.0	2.9	1.2
BRS Parcels	12.1	12.2	12.8	5.4	3.8
Pickfords	11.7	12.2	11.3	11.1	9.3

[a] BRS General, BRS Parcels and Pickfords are all part of the same group.

Source: Thomson and Hunter, (1973), p. 252.

firms. BRS' figures are generally lower than those of the private firms (Table 3.2), although its overall performance was respectable.

Pryke (1981) compared the NFC's net margins after depreciation costs with those of a combination of the Transport Development Group's general and special haulage, and United Carriers, one of Britain's largest parcels businesses. The two groups then derived about the same proportion of revenue from parcels. The NFC's profit margin in 1979 was 4.8 per cent compared to 9.7 per cent for the private group.

Modernisation: 1970-9

Over the entire period from 1968 to 1979, the NFC gradually reorganised into a commercially efficient, road freight-based business unit. Staff numbers were reduced nearly 50 per cent, from 66,000 in 1968 to 34,000 in 1979. The number of vehicles was also reduced from 29,000 to 18,500 in the same period. Volume in parcels contracted by some 45 per cent, and general haulage became a smaller part of non-parcels revenue. Meanwhile, the NFC's share of the road freight transport market settled at approximately 7 per cent. The contraction in capacity created high numbers of redundancies, particularly in the period 1976–9 when several depots were closed. As a result revenue per employee increased by 40 per cent in real terms, from £10,500 in 1968 to over £14,000 in 1979. In 1979 a modest profit of £2 million was achieved on a turnover of £400 million, the first since 1968.

An important contributor to the successful restructuring of the NFC was the sale of assets as a buffer against financial collapse. When the NFC was established, net assets were valued at approximately £100 million including excess capacity in vehicles and many outmoded and unsuitable depots in the property portfolio. The potential for the sale of substantial properties was acknowledged in the early 1970s, and many were sold in the capital crisis of the mid-1970s. By 1976, the value of net assets had been reduced to £65 million, a substantial reduction in view of the price inflation in the period:

> This feat of management, combining the profitable sale of assets with trading losses, such that the net assets of the business actually declined during a period of substantial contraction . . . is the most notable feature that strikes anybody looking at the Corporation's record from 1969 to 1976 . . . the business has been living off its assets, selling buildings, reducing its lorry fleet, reducing the numbers employed until it can find a level of operation where it is both competitive and efficient. (Redwood, 1980: pp. 144–7)

Given poor capitalisation, inherited burdens and high commercial priorities, senior management of the NFC had to find the finance to continue operations. The reorganisation of property assets, including the disposal of outmoded sites, was as necessary as reducing overmanning and diversifying into new product markets.

Although integration was no longer a goal after 1970, the NFC was still burdened with other political commitments which prevented the speedy movement towards commercial efficiency. The most serious financial problem was in parcels which accounted for 45 per cent of revenue. In particular, the 1968 Act transferred the British Railways Board's highly unprofitable road freight activities to the NFC. In 1968 the Sundries Division of BRB (renamed National Carriers) lost some £20 million on a turnover of £25 million, and Freightliners lost £2 million. In addition, the NFC was burdened with high manning levels. Some 25,000 of its 66,000 employees after the transfer were ex-railwaymen who were guaranteed the same conditions under the NFC as they had enjoyed under the British Railways Board.

The 1968 Act called for a payment of £60 million in subsidies to the NFC over five years to compensate for National Carriers. However, these subsidies were phased out in 1973 because of good trading conditions and a considerable reduction in excess manpower and vehicles, which took the NFC into an overall trading profit in 1972. Further improvements in trading profits were achieved in 1973. In 1974 the new Labour government noted the NFC's progress, its good and imaginative management, and its emphasis on quality as opposed to volume service.

Despite the NFC's encouraging start, it was still constrained by its responsibilities under the Transport Act 1968. After deducting interest repayments, the NFC did not make an overall profit until 1978. Both

National Carriers and the older British Road Services parcels network, renamed Roadline in the mid-1970s, were consistent loss-makers.[15] Furthermore, the capital constraints of the 1968 Act restricted the Corporation's ability to shift its business away from general transport towards more specialised services with more stable demand, such as food distribution.[16] Thomson and Hunter (1973) argued that the NFC's existing range of clients already stabilised its business through the trade cycle. This sanguine view was disproved by the NFC's experience in the mid-1970s. Lacking capital to support full modernisation, the Corporation could not sustain the momentum of growth in the mid-1970s when the economy declined. Heavy losses were incurred in 1974 and 1975, with total losses in 1975 of some £31 million.

The NFC's management were slow to modernise their own practices. In the early 1970s 'its subsidiaries were run as personal fiefs by managing directors whose stewardship could not be seriously questioned as long as they retained the confidence of the Corporation's chairman. In addition, some very poor appointments were made' (Pryke, 1981: p. 126). Among the most serious problems was a lingering commitment to defending high volume in road freight transport, which often interfered with managing in the best commercial interests of the NFC as a group.

Still more damaging was an ill-fated diversification in the early 1970s. A massive expansion into Europe was expected to provide 50 per cent of NFC's revenue within five years. Hurried acquisitions were made, often of unprofitable concerns. In 1975 the European venture cost £11 million in losses.

Recovery: 1976–9

In 1976 senior management was changed. The majority of the new appointments had had outside industrial or financial experience before joining the NFC. Peter Thompson, who later led the buyout, became Chief Executive (Operations). The government then provided the NFC with financial support which began a dramatic recovery. Between 1976 and 1981 the workforce was almost halved from 50,000 and real revenue per employee grew at 3 per cent per annum. A grant of £22 million was made to finance cash flow deficits with a promise to act on the NFC's inherited problems and weak capital base.

The new commercially orientated operational management pursued modernisation with greater vigour. They accelerated the policy of diversification into more profitable and less vulnerable specialised services, including cold storage, specialised distribution, waste management, shipping and forwarding, household removals and travel businesses to insulate the NFC from the business cycle. The NFC's profitability also improved steadily in the late 1970s.

The Transport Act 1978 reorganised the NFC's capital structure, which had collapsed in the mid-1970s when the Corporation had been forced to borrow in order to service prior debts. The Corporation's capital debt was reduced by 50 per cent to £100 million and it was given capital expenditure grants of up to £15 million for National Carriers. The Act also transferred financial responsibility for funding certain pension fund deficiencies and travel concessions to ex-rail employees to the government.

The 1978 Act returned Freightliners to British Rail. That was a disappointment to the Corporation's Board for the 10 years that the NFC had controlled Freightliners, it had been reorganised effectively and was contributing profitable revenue. Nevertheless, the NFC emerged from the reconstruction of 1978 in a sounder financial condition, able to continue modernisation whilst rationalising unprofitable parcels and general services.

Management were encouraged to operate NFC like a private firm by a 1977 Conservative Party policy document (Fowler, 1977) which hinted at privatisation should the party return to power. After 1976, an important component in the NFC's modernisation programme was an attempt to encourage a more participative style of management. This shift was difficult to implement, particularly in the traditional road haulage centres with a convention of autocratic management practices. Nevertheless, in 1977 with the cooperation of the trade unions, the National Freight Corporation (1977) circulated a document to management which outlined ways of improving communication with employees and the dissemination of information. In 1980 the NFC moved towards performance-related pay bonuses for clerical employees. The focus on local initiatives resulted also in the decentralisation of collective bargaining over pay rates to Group and company level. This approach was intended to provide employment packages more relevent to the particular operating circumstances and needs of the different activities within the Corporation.

Despite the NFC's recovery in the late 1970s, its capital structure continued to constrain growth and product development. Given the competitive environment in which the NFC had to operate, the conventional funding arrangements of nationalised industries were too inflexible.[17] In response, a 1976 Labour Party document on transport committed the government to increased nationalisation of road freight activities. The Corporation itself made a statement expressing its alternative proposals for the future of the organisation:

> The trend towards specialisation is evident throught the NFC's operating subsidiaries. It would be aided, and the achievement

of complete viability brought closer, by more flexible financing arrangements than the fixed interest loan capital structure within which we are obliged to work. This could be achieved by replacing part of the fixed interest financing by public or private equity capital. While not reducing our obligations this would enable us to make our investment and time our distribution of 'dividend' in line with economic and business trends. (National Freight Corporation, Annual Report, 1977)

Given a strong economic case for privatising the NFC, why did a buyout rather than a conventional sale result? The relatively weak economic performance of the Corporation required a pragmatic solution. The NFC data supports the hypothesis that under a wide set of circumstances in privatisation, the pragmatic interests of the main protagonists may coincide to produce a successful buyout.

The following sections describe the processes and timing of decisions relating to the sale of the NFC. Evidence is based on company archival data, secondary sources and interviews with members of the NFC, the Transport and General Workers' Union (TGWU), representatives from political parties, personnel from other nationalised industries and managers from Barclays Development Capital.

The buyout: June 1979–January 1981

The government

The years 1979 to 1983 saw some significant changes in the Conservative Party. The radical strategies of the New Right necessitated a different approach to decision-making, as manifested in Margaret Thatcher's style of conviction politics, which was marked by determination and consistency in implementing strategic commitments and party policy.

The appointment of ministers and spokesmen in the relevant departments (public sector enterprises were concentrated in six industries or sectors) took on a strategic significance. Much would depend on their commitment to privatisation of state industries. Undoubtedly, detailed formulation of an unprecedented programme is a complex practical process requiring the learning of new skills with additional problems to overcome during implementation. But the political appointments may determine whether the desire to tackle the difficulties exists.

In the late 1970s the Conservative Party's spokesman on Transport, Norman Fowler, was highly committed to the new radical strategies of the Conservative Party. In a Conservative Party policy document on Transport, Fowler (1977) declared that there was no longer any strategic need to have a public sector road freight transport industry, since the traditional post-war objective of integrating road and rail transport had dissipated. He suggested that a future Conservative government would separate National Carriers from the rest of the NFC in order to allow the latter to grow and be profitable. Given this position, the paper continued, 'we would aim to achieve substantial private investment in the corporation'. However, it was unclear about how this investment was to be achieved. Options to be considered included joint ventures with private industry, and the sale of NFC's subsidiaries to the private sector. Fowler's 'preferred solution, however, [was] to seek private investment in the NFC, and provide a corporation similar . . . in make-up to British Petroleum' (Fowler, 1977). In other words, a future Conservative government would retain a majority interest in the NFC and sell the balance to the private sector.

The Conservative Party's 1979 election Manifesto included a pledge to denationalise the NFC: 'we aim to sell shares in the National Freight Corporation to the general public in order to achieve a substantial private investment in it' (Conservative Party, 1979). The NFC was one of the few industries specifically mentioned for privatisation, suggesting that it was a high priority. However, according to Norman Fowler, then the Secretary of State for Transport, 'it [the privatisation of the NFC] was not a major issue in the House of Commons and neither was it a major consideration within the Party . . . I just wanted to finish the job.'[18] The government's legal preparations proceeded. An enabling law was passed in preparation for the sale. The Transport Act 1980 converted the NFC's capital structure from that of a loan-based public corporation to an equity-based limited company. All equity was vested in the Department of Transport. This enabled (but did not oblige) the minister to sell shares. The NFC's debts were extinguished and constraints on directors' salaries and areas of business activity were removed. The Act also committed the government to fund most of the NFC's pensions fund liability. This issue was very important as some £40 million would be taken from the sale receipts to fund part of the deficiencies.[19]

In preparing for the sale of the NFC the government appointed the merchant bank J. Henry Schroder Wagg (Schroders) to advise the NFC on valuation. In July 1979 the company was estimated to be worth between £57 million and £90 million. It was assumed that a flotation would not take place before mid-1981 and that neither the market conditions nor the NFC's performance forecasts would change. In the event, the latter assumption proved false.

Because of the derived demand nature of road freight transport, the NFC depends heavily upon the prosperity of the general economy. Consequently, the severe recession which affected the British economy in the

47

early 1980s substantially reduced the NFC's contracts and profit forecasts. Further, in September 1980, only weeks after its incorporation under the Transport Act, the NFC suffered a major setback when it lost the British Railways Express Parcels Service (BREPS) contract. The NFC had been the subcontractor for the supply of drivers and vehicles for this service. This activity, the NFC's single largest contract, had provided some £25 million profitable revenue per annum. Overall in 1980 a trading loss of £7.5 million was incurred and extensive redundancies had to be made. A full flotation in 1981 now seemed unlikely.

The loss of the British Railways Express Parcels Service came just two weeks after the completion of incorporation. The government had asked the newly formed NFC Board to prepare for flotation on the Stock Exchange. This move would have secured an acceptable price for the government and allowed it to widen share ownership among managers, employees and small investors. Then it became clear that the real improvements in the NFC's performance since the mid-1970s would not be reflected in the recession-affected figures for 1980; any sale price would be low, and a delay seemed imminent. In January 1981 Schroders formally confirmed a lower estimate of value and advised against an early flotation. The bank also suggested that the earliest possible sale date would be summer 1982 or early 1983, and that the sale price would be closer to £50 million.

Given their election Manifesto commitment and a Secretary of State for Transport – Norman Fowler – who was keen to achieve a successful privatisation, it became increasingly plausible that the government would consider alternative ways of disposing of the NFC. The preference would be for a sale to a single buyer, to avoid the political and administrative problems associated with dividing the organisation among several buyers.

The National Freight Corporation

The NFC Board was initially ambivalent about privatisation. Release from financial and pay constraints would be welcomed, but there were concerns about the marketability of the company. Losses in the parcels sections and general haulage made the NFC an unattractive investment as a group. Further, the company's large and lucrative property portfolio would be attractive to asset-stripping investors unconcerned about securing the NFC's future. It seemed that the method of sale would be crucial in determining whether the NFC continued to modernise and grow as a group, or whether it contracted, rationalised and shed jobs, or even fragmented.

The government had not ruled out the possibility of selling the NFC piecemeal, retaining the undesirable activities whilst divesting the most desirable. The 1977 policy document had referred to the possibility of dismantling the group, and that option was considered by the government after the election victory. Norman Fowler later recalled, 'I came to the conclusion that NFC was a good business trying to get out. There was no logical reason for it to be in the public sector . . . ' (McLachlan, 1983: p. 87). This view appeared acceptable to the NFC's senior management. However, Fowler continued, 'indeed there was no logical reason for the NFC at all: very few people outside of those directly involved were even aware of NFC's existence. People identified with the operating subsidiaries, but not with the parent Corporation' (McLachlan, 1983: p. 87). Thus, there was good reason for people in certain parts of the organisation to be concerned about job security.

In May 1979 the NFC's senior management considered that four options were available to the government: (i) the sale of a minority stake public flotation of the NFC as it existed; (iii) an offer for sale of the NFC minus its loss-makers; and (iv) the piecemeal sale of the desirable parts of the NFC. Of the four strategies, the Board judged the second to be most politically expedient. Because of the NFC's financial forecasts for 1979, however, an immediate sale would require a substantial discount on asset value. The forecasts for 1980 would support a price closer to the real asset value, but that would require a delay of the sale until the end of 1981. Such a lengthy period of uncertainty might destabilise relationships with customers and suppliers. The NFC Board therefore considered that both the government and the NFC might be forced to examine other options.

As overall trading conditions worsened during 1979-80 this possibility became increasingly plausible. Following incorporation the balance on the NFC Board was shifted towards the executives, who constituted five of the twelve Board members. After the loss of the British Railways Express Parcels Service, they became concerned that a delay in the sale of NFC would increase the danger of dismantling. As the balance of power on the Board shifted towards the executives, the determination to maintain the NFC's unity increased. The non-executive Board members, however, were still required to pursue the interests of their shareholders, the government.

After the completion of the Transport Act 1980, a difference of interests emerged between executive and non-executive Board members. Against a backcloth of a boom in management buyouts in 1980-1 (*Financial Times Survey*, 1981), the executive Board members began to consider the possibility of a management buyout bid for the NFC. Thus the initial impetus for the buyout came from management's desire to avoid an unacceptable disposal which would have threatened their own careers and exposed the NFC to asset-stripping new owners. According to Sir Peter Thompson, Chairman of the NFC, the senior managers began to think that what was likely to happen to the NFC is what subsequently happened to British Transport Hotels which were broken up and sold to third parties. That gets you into a situation of: 'God, what does this mean for us?' We sat around, about six or seven of us, and talked about this. At some stage I said, 'Why the hell don't we do a management buyout?' And that is the concept we sold to Norman Fowler. (Interview between authors and Sir Peter Thompson, December 1987)

The staff buyout phase: January 1981–January 1982

It was not at all clear that a successful staff buyout would be possible. The pioneering nature of the consortium's intentions created numerous unprecedented legal and technical problems. The fact that these were overcome whilst the consortium was being built reflects the determination of the buyout leaders, and a coincidence of interests among many different groups.

The government

The government's enthusiastic support for the management-led buyout attempt after June 1981 can be viewed as an indication of its relief at finding a solution to the problem of how to sell the NFC. Since the loss of the British Railways Express Parcels Service contract, the government's political options had narrowed. The favoured solution, a public flotation, was not feasible until 1983, and a management-led consortium offered several advantages over the other options. The remaining conventional methods of sale involved fragmenting the NFC which could not satisfy the government's disparate objectives. Selling parts piecemeal would threaten the employment level in the firm as the head office was eliminated. If the parcels and general haulage units could be sold, further job losses were likely, while the sale of only the profitable units would leave a rump of undesirables in the public sector. Further, as the Transport Act 1980 had committed the government to fund a large part of the pension deficiency, fragmentation would have resulted in a net revenue loss to the government. Moreover, a piecemeal sale would involve lengthy and difficult negotiations with different bidders.[20] A sale to a single buyer with acceptable interests in the NFC was the ideal.

The government also had to be perceived to be receiving the best possible sale price. The intensity of public and parliamentary scrutiny (through the Public Accounts Committee and the Treasury) of privatisation efforts has varied. In 1981, however, the government was sensitive to accusations of impropriety, since a 16.5 per cent discount on the sale of British Aerospace in February had led to the issue being oversubscribed three-and-a-half times. Discounts on sales were not precluded, but the government would have to show that (i) there was open competition for bidders, (ii) the best price offered was being considered most seriously, and (iii) any discount was not going to speculators.

In this environment, the buyout consortium approached the secretary of state in June 1981 to request that only their proposal be considered by the government. Its consent would have removed one element of uncertainty in the consortium's preparations, facilitating communications with the workforce. He did not agree, however, since the government had to be seen to be attaining the best possible deal. Yet the government would not simply sell to the highest bidder. For example, foreign bidders were unlikely to be received favourably. In early 1981 an oblique approach from a Swiss merchant bank received little attention. The buyout consortium remained the only bidder until a late bid was received in autumn 1981, by which time the buyout had been agreed by most parties.[21]

The government also had to safeguard its image with respect to wider share ownership. Although its full extent did not emerge until later, there are indications that the number of small investors in privatised companies declined significantly in the year after flotation. The number of shareholders in British Aerospace dropped 83 per cent during the first year after privatisation; the number of small investors fell 93 per cent, to 3,300. At Cable and Wireless, which was privatised in October 1981, the number of shareholders fell by some 80 per cent, to 26,000, in the first year (Trades Union Congress, 1985).

The consortium

After their initial discussions, the executive directors rapidly shifted to the concept of a staff buyout involving wider employee financial participation. Why did this group not simply attempt a management buyout?

The NFC's Chief Executive and the buyout's chief organiser, Peter Thompson, had set his sights on a new form of industrial enterprise which got 'everybody involved'. In his view

> unless we could keep a very substantial part of this business in
> equity for the employees it wasn't a classical buyout . . . I
> suppose there was the realisation that if you could somehow
> get everyone involved with a piece of the action some of our
> problems, which have been pretty deep rooted, particularly
> union problems, would go away and we'd get rid of the 'them
> and us' syndrome. That was the vision that we had when we

started. (Interview between authors and Sir Peter Thompson, December 1987)

Thompson's 'vision' had its roots in his disillusionment with socialism:

at university where I read economics I became very involved with the feeling that society wasn't fairly organised and there wasn't enough planning. So, I became a classical socialist. But then I became disillusioned with the monoliths which were set up. The nationalised industries which were supposed to reflect a feeling of common ownership became the worst kind of monolith. (Interview between authors and Sir Peter Thompson, December 1987)

The fact that they failed in a crucial social welfare function affected Thompson:

there were more jobs being lost and a harsher kind of management style than one encountered in private industry. For example, we were state owned and we did nothing for pensioners. We gave our pensioners a pension but that was the end of it. We had no structure by which we could visit them or see to their needs after they'd left. I increasingly became disillusioned with the planned economy and the global approach to socialism. At the same time I recognised that inside conservatism there was the dynamics which could get a society moving. If you get the incentives right all the rest would follow. We are owned for the benefit of the people who work for the company. And that turns me on. It satisfies people's natural greed and also satisfies their need to be involved. It also satisfies the philosophical concept that if you're creating wealth you should share it. (Interview between authors and Sir Peter Thompson, December 1987)

There were also structural reasons for wider share ownership. In April 1981 the consortium approached Barclays Merchant Bank (BMB), which eventually led the other banks in negotiations with the NFC. In preliminary discussions the Organising Committee of the Consortium suggested that the NFC's size made it unlikely that a small management team could raise sufficient finance to purchase the company. If participation were restricted to management, only a limited institutional buyout would be possible, with management holding a minority equity position. This option would probably have left the Group vulnerable to aggressive bidders in the future. Additionally, it was felt that an employee buyout would have greater political appeal than a buyout restricted to management. This consideration may have persuaded the government to sell the company intact at a discounted rate. Finally, it seems likely that Barclays Merchant Bank strongly favoured an extensive employee buyout on the grounds that the participation of employees would win the commitment of the workforce to the change. Employee financial participation also spread risks and provided greater security for any loan finance the banks provided.

The role of Barclays Merchant Bank in the construction of the buyout is examined more closely below. The bank's preference for employee share participation happily coincided with the views of the executive directors. However, the sensitive nature of the buyout option prevented a full Board discussion until March 1981. Before then, the executive directors produced a confidential document which presented the case for a staff buyout.[22] It argued that the government's political commitment to the privatisation of the NFC did not relate to financial considerations. But for any sale to be politically acceptable the price could not be derisory. This was a crucial factor favouring a sale to a management-led consortium. After the pensions fund deficiency had been paid the governement would receive a very small amount for the sale. The document argued that the government might respond favourably to an early disposal, at the same price, to a management-led consortium. A scheme that extended the invitation of equity participation to the entire workforce would be encouraging an important government priority, namely wider share ownership. Furthermore, an employee-owned NFC would be difficult for a future Labour government to renationalise. Thus, the document argued, an employee buyout might be the most acceptable solution to the delayed sale for the government. For the buyers the purchase would secure, temporarily at least, the existing structure of the group whilst employee shareholding would give an incentive to make a success of the company.

The paper concluded that because of the government's commitment to fund the pensions deficiency and the poor state of the economy, which prevented a conventional flotation, the government might look favourably upon a management-led staff buyout that satisfied four conditions: (i) it offered the opportunity for an early disposal of the entire NFC; (ii) it provided approximately the same net proceeds as a public flotation; (iii) it involved a cross-section of the workforce; and (iv) it could demonstrate management commitment.

Five principles of a buyout were laid down in the document:
(i)   Control of the new company would be vested in the management and ultimately with the employees.
(ii) A minority equity stake would be extended to outside investors.

(iii) The structure would enable an eventual stock market quotation, if required.
(iv) Senior management would be expected to participate and share purchase would be a condition of employment for new management recruits in the future.
(v) Shares would be transferable, but only between employees through a share trust, which received independent share valuations.

The case for a management-led buyout was presented to the Board in March, along with a tentative suggestion for the financial structure of the purchase. Some £5 million equity finance would be raised by staff and management and a further £50 million would be raised in loan finance to fund the pensions deficiency. At this point the division between executive and non-executive directors was crystallised. The Board gave cautious approval to the executives to proceed with the idea.

Following the Board's agreement in principle, the executive directors had to seek a wider base of support for the buyout. Looking inside first, they consulted senior management confidentially. This small group was composed of the operational directors of the main NFC divisions and the Head of Communications Services who was later to play a key role in informing the workforce of the buyout proposal. This group gave enthusiastic support to the plan and subsequently combined with the executive directors to spearhead the consortium as the thirteen-member Organising Committee.

The Organising Committee then approached Schroders for approval to proceed along the lines of the financial structure suggested to the Board. Schroders expressed doubts about the ability to raise £5 million in equity. They indicated the committee might proceed, but refused to support a buyout at this stage.

The secretary of state was approached in April. Although agreeing in principle, he required feasibility studies to be undertaken before he would give his support. He also advised the NFC that he wished to complete a sale by July 1982.

The caution shown by Schroders and the government was understandable given the unprecedented scale of the proposed purchase. Now the organising committee had the onus of presenting proposals and formulating a package, which required them to raise finance and evaluate support within the organisation. Discussions with Barclays Merchant Bank opened in April. By early June, BMB suggested that a highly geared package with equity of approximately £5 to £7 million and a loan of some £50 million, preferably backed by securities, would achieve a successful buyout with majority control resting with the workforce. Now communications with the workforce, although still confidential, could proceed. First, however, the top 130 managers in the Group were consulted in a meeting in early June about the potential for such an ambitious scheme. The Organising Committee received a very positive response including an estimate that some £5 million could be raised from the entire NFC workforce. Following this meeting, the Organising Committee approached the secretary of state for final approval to proceed.

On 18 June the buyout was launched in four important ways. At the parliamentary level, the secretary of state announced his support for the buyout in the House of Commons. His statement also served the purpose of making it known that the government had an acceptable option, so other parties considering a bid should decide what they wanted to do. Of more importance for securing the necessary financial support was the joint press conference between senior NFC representatives and Barclays Merchant Bank held on the same day. BMB was still nervous about the deal, given the legal difficulties in organising security for the loans, but their participation at the press conference was an important indication of support for the consortium.[23]

The buyout was also announced to employees in a printed letter given to the entire workforce. However, detailed discussions and presentations did not begin until August 1981. The fourth communication was to the main trade unions represented at the NFC.[24] Given the general hostility of the labour movement to privatisation, it is not surprising that the initial reaction was negative. Only the United Road Transport Union (URTU), the smallest union, supported employee ownership by way of an employee buyout. The remaining unions objected to the sale of public assets in principle, and in particular feared the effects of the sale on employment levels, and terms and conditions of employment.

Interviews with regional TGWU officials at the NFC suggested that greater trade union support for the proposals could have been mobilised if the consortium had been willing to form a producer cooperative. A proposal for a cooperative structure was mooted among some union leaders, but was never presented to the Organising Committee. The feeling was that this arrangement would not have been acceptable to the financial institutions. Nor was it acceptable to the Organising Committee's senior executives. Peter Thompson emphasised the distinction between the consortium's idea (a commercially motivated NFC with worker-owners, but a conventional management) and a Meriden-type solution, a reference to the ailing motorcycle manufacturer which had been converted to a producer cooperative in 1975. The latter option would lead the NFC 'down the slippery slope to mediocrity', he felt.

The unions considered bargaining for the allocation of a block of equity as beneficial trustees for their members. Again no proposals were ever presented to the Organising Committee as feeling in union circles was that the funds could not have been raised. In addition the financial institutions would probably have resisted or withdrawn. The union's eventual policy reflected the relative weakness of trade unions during this period. The NUR, TSSA and AUEW concluded that given the government's commitment to privatising the NFC, a buyout involving a high level of employee share participation was the most acceptable option. The TGWU, however, announced their opposition to privatisation, advised their members not to invest and remained committed to renationalisation on the return of a Labour government.

Given the TGWU's opposition, the consortium's presentation to employees became very important. In late June a series of six large regional meetings were held with the NFC's 2,300 managers. Two-way consultation and dissemination of information resulted in a positive show of strength for the buyout proposals. Communicating with non-management employees, particularly manual employees, was more difficult. One problem was that the majority of the 23,500 workforce related primarily to their local company or even a depot. Few perceived themselves as employed by the NFC. In addition, the effort had to overcome employees' inexperience with share ownership and the continuing uncertainty over the eventual financial structure. The consortium employed sophisticated communications techniques including the use of videos at local promotion meetings. Care was taken to explain the concept of share ownership, what the buyout meant and the fact that share ownership did not affect rights as employees.

The Civil Service

In the summer of 1979 the Department of Transport set up a working party with representatives from its own Policy and Finance directorates, the NFC, Schroders, and solicitors to coordinate and implement the privatisation of the NFC (McLachlan, 1983: p. 90). One notable omission was the Treasury. In the early stages of its privatisation programme, the government was still learning about the most effective way to administer sales. As each candidate for sale was announced, preparations were made on an *ad hoc* basis. During this phase the Treasury's influence varied. It was only later, when the Treasury evolved a more systematic response to privatisation, that it was represented on all working parties.

Because the Treasury did not participate in the NFC's preparations for sale, policy matters had a relative advantage in trade-offs against finance. This perhaps explains the early incorporation of the NFC as a limited company. The Transport Act 1980 required that the NFC's status be transferred not long after the passage of the Act. The Treasury and Finance Division were concerned that the early incorporation left the NFC in a financial limbo. Financing would have to come from the private sector, which still viewed the NFC as a public sector enterprise. The NFC could probably have borrowed as if its loans were underwritten by the government. This raised the question: what would happen if the NFC's performance deteriorated even further during 1981? Would the government assist?

In the view of others, including the NFC, these concerns were outweighed by the early advantages of early incorporation. Because of the company's patchy performance history, it seemed desirable for the NFC to have time to establish a successful trading track record. The relative autonomy of a lengthy incorporation was the least objectionable way of doing so.

Financial institutions

Among the professional advisers employed by the government in the privatisation process probably the most influential are the merchant banks. They are often closely involved in the organisational process and advise upon topics of critical political importance.

Schroders was appointed in the summer of 1979 to advise both the NFC and the government. In July 1979 they produced a document based on the government's working plans.[25] Schroders' influence is reflected in the subsequent implementation of many of the proposals in this paper, despite the unorthodox eventual sale. They recommended that the entire NFC capital debt of £100 million be extinguished for equity and that the new company have a lower gearing ratio.[26] Schroders suggested that if the NFC was to be floated its Board should resemble that of a Stock Exchange company; for example, there should be a balance between executive and non-executive directors, and the company should not be burdened with commitments that any other Stock Exchange firm would not have.[27]

After the Organising Committee voiced its intention to attempt a buyout, Schroders' role changed. Although it gave its consent to the consortium to prepare plans, it could no longer operate in the interests of both the government and the NFC. Schroders was eventually appointed by the government to complete the transaction on its behalf. This experience probably stood Schroders in good stead for the future as it was later appointed by the government to advise on the sales of the Associated British Ports and Jaguar Cars.

Much has been made of the non-suitability of Schroders' branch of banking to the needs of the consortium. For example, one of Schroders' negotiators at the NFC said, in reference to the Barclays loan package: 'We certainly would not have been prepared to put together that sort of loan package. It's not our type of banking. In a situation where clearing bank money is going to be a critical factor, then obviously the proposition is far better suited to someone like BMB than ourselves' (see McLachlan, 1983: p. 72).

Possibly, however, Schroders simply did not consider a buyout with staff control feasible. The eventual sale package certainly ignored Schroders' 1979 recommendation that the NFC should not be highly geared, so it may be that Schroders was unwilling rather than unable to raise the finance for the consortium's proposal.

In any case the Organising Committee was obliged to look elsewhere for finance. In late April it approached Barclays Merchant Bank. After discussions of the NFC's commercial prospects, its managerial quality, the pensions problems and property portfolio, they agreed on a package in which BMB held a small minority equity stake. Most of the return on investment was expected to be in the form of interest on loans. Given the high interest rates in 1981–2 and the high gearing ratio of the package, the NFC was expected to make high interest repayments, an indication perhaps of BMB's confidence in the NFC's prospects.

Why was BMB willing to raise the finance for the deal? Clearly the support of a clearing bank parent was an advantage. Moreover, as a new subsidiary of Barclays, BMB was attempting to break into the market with a high profile deal. However, there were also sound financial reasons. BMB's approval of any package was based on the satisfaction of certain conditions: firstly, that employees, pensioners and families could raise at least £4.5 million in share purchases, with the banks underwriting the balance if necessary; secondly, that banks had a 10 to 20 per cent equity stake; thirdly, that the thirteen senior managers, the Organising Committee, could raise £250,000 for equity; fourthly, that the 1,250 most senior managers could raise £625,000 for equity. BMB would then lend approximately £50 million to the consortium to finance the pensions deficiency, and permit an overdraft facility of up to £25 million.

A major problem for the consortium, which continued during the communications exercise, was that doubts still existed about the structure and financing of the buyout and the final arrangements that would be employed. A number of problems remained unresolved until close to the sale date. Perhaps the largest problem was that, in return for the £50 million loan, Barclays Bank wanted security in the form of property valued at £75 million. This demand presented two legal difficulties. Firstly, the NFC's property assets were then still technically owned by the subsidiaries so that negotiations with subsidiary Boards would be required. Secondly, and more importantly, the Companies Act 1948 prohibited the purchase of a company with its own assets. Consequently, a company's property assets could not be used as security. A Companies Bill, then under consideration by Parliament, contained sections amending the 1948 Act which would have allowed the consortium to give such security, but it was not certain that the new legislation would be passed.[28] It seems plausible that the Organising Committee delayed the purchase in order to wait for the new leglislation. By November 1981, it became clear that the Companies Bill would be passed speedily, perhaps in the knowledge that the NFC was waiting for it.

Problems about property remained, the major difficulty being valuation. NFC's valuations were based on the use-value of sites, whereas the banks employed the market value. Following a compromise which favoured the consortium's valuations, some 250 sites were put up as security to the value of £76.5 million. In return a medium-term loan of £51 million was repayable in ten years commencing in 1984. A trading facility of up to £30 million would also be available. A notable feature of this agreement was that it valued the best 25 per cent of the NFC's property sites at almost 1.5 times the sale price of the entire company. The final sale price of £53.5 million reflected the market value of the Group in February 1982, but grossly undervalued its real asset value. This factor has undeniably contributed to the outstanding capital growth of the NFC since the change of ownership. It also suggests why the government may have been so reluctant to sell the NFC to any other bidder, particularly as the net return after funding the pensions liabilities was so small; and why the financial institutions were willing to provide funding for a highly geared package during a period of high interest rates.

The government finally agreed to sell the newly incorporated National Freight Company Ltd in October 1981 although doubts remained about the exact property and pension fund deficiency valuations. A new public company, the National Freight Consortium, would take over the National Freight Company Ltd. Following the agreement on property valuations, the National Freight Consortium plc was formally incorporated with an authorised share capital valuation of £8.5 million, at the end of 1981. The details of the financial package were not complete until December, when profit forecasts were downgraded. It was only then that the Prospectus inviting employees, their families and pensioners to participate could be distributed.

The buyout package

The financing of the package was clearly presented in the Prospectus (see

Table 3.3. *The financing of the purchase of the National Freight Company*

		£m		£m
A	Bank loans	51.0	Purchase price	53.5
B	Short-term BMB loans to finance employee loan scheme and transaction costs	4.0	Employee loan scheme	3.0
C	Equity		Transaction costs	1.0
	'A' shareholders	6.2		
	'B' shareholders	1.3		
	Total	62.5	Total	57.5

Table 3.3). The sale price of £53.5 million was raised from several sources. Fifty-one million pounds came from bank loans to the consortium. Up to 6.2 million ordinary 'A' shares, representing 82.5 per cent of total ordinary share capital, were sold to employees, their families and pensioners. Up to 1.32 million ordinary 'B' shares, representing the remaining 17.5 per cent of ordinary share capital, were sold to the banks in the consortium. BMB also provided approximately £4 million in short-term loans to fund the Employee Loan Scheme and to pay the transactions costs. A total of £62.5 million was raised to finance the deal of which £53.5 million was used to pay for the National Freight Company plc and £4 million for costs and the loan scheme. The prospectus also stated that it expected to pay a dividend of 7.5p per £1 share for the year up to October 1982.

The financial group led by BMB had agreed to lend some £51 million in return for some £1.3 million worth of shares. A £30 million overdraft facility was also available from Barclays Bank. In return the equity structure reflected the financial institutions' desire for some control. While the 'A' and 'B' shareholders had equal rights to the payment of dividends, 'B' shareholders had the automatic right to appoint a director to the Board of the consortium as long as they held a minimum 5 per cent equity stake, some £37,500. Unlike the rest of the Board, the 'B' shareholders' director was not subject to re-election on a rotation basis. 'B' shareholders could also veto any increase in the number of 'A' shares above a small agreed annual figure set aside for new employees.

Eligibility was restricted to employees, their families and pensioners. The inclusion of pensioners increased the number of those eligible by some 50 per cent to a total of 44,000. However, only employees could use the employee loan scheme. (Up to £200 could be borrowed interest-free, repayable within twelve months to be deducted from wages and salaries.) No individual could buy more than £100,000 worth of shares.

The marketability and valuation of shares were important issues. No stock market quotation existed to determine a price, nor any market mechanism for valuation. An independent share trust was set up to handle transfers between buyers and sellers and to seek an independent valuation on the shares between two and four times a year. Shares could be transferred through the share trust only on four appointed days a year (Dealing days).

The Prospectus also clarified the nature of the organisation. Firstly, it was not a cooperative. Each share carried one vote. The NFC would retain a conventional management structure, although communications with shareholders would be developed. Employees could be active policy-makers, but only as shareholders.

Secondly, there was no obligation to invest when joining the NFC or any of its subsidiaries, nor any obligation to sell when leaving under normal circumstances. Although the Organising Committee had discussed requiring managers to invest, this condition was eventually dropped.

Thirdly, the Prospectus and the communications campaign in general stressed that status in the NFC was unrelated to whether the employee invested or not. Being a shareholder did not guarantee a job or prevent redundancy. This was an important statement given the fears in certain parts of the organisation that a sale to an aggressive bidder would mean asset stripping and job losses. Confidentiality concerning who owned shares was both essential and encouraged by the consortium. Fourthly, the Board agreed not to make any proposals for public flotation before February 1987, five years after the buyout.

The buyout's initial success was reflected in the response to the invitation to invest. The initial offer of shares was oversubscribed by more than 800,000 when it closed in February 1982. Requests for up to £600 per person were met in full, but larger bids were scaled down by 17 per cent. Over 10,000 individuals bought shares of whom approximately 1,300 were pensioners. Therefore, some 9,000 employees and their families invested, about 40 per cent of the entire workforce. Little is known about the distribution of shares. However, on the assumption that all 2,000 of the NFC's managers did invest, it can be estimated that at least 30 per cent of non-managerial employees made some investment in February 1982.

4

The employment investment decision: issues

Introduction

A successful transfer of ownership depends on a coincidence of interests between buyer and seller. A seller may favour an employee buyout over more conventional forms of divestment if it promises a speedier completion of the transaction or if financial markets seem likely to demand a heavily discounted price. But what about the buyer's interests? Why does an individual employee decide to invest in a buyout situation? When a buyout seems the only way to prevent closure of the firm, employees may invest to save their jobs. But in other situations, a desire for financial gain seems to be the predominant motive.

Ownership involves several kinds of risk as well as potential benefits. Firstly, an investment in his own company concentrates the employee's economic risk (see, for example, Samuelson, 1977). Prudence suggests that any employee equity investment should be made outside the company in which he works; otherwise a failed investment may mean loss of both capital and employment.

Secondly, in all employee financial participation schemes, the revenue produced by the enterprise is shared in some way between capital and labour. As a consequence, labour shares in the risks of fluctuations in that revenue. Company revenue and performance depend on many factors besides employee performance, so that the employee-owner who increases his individual efforts will not necessarily be rewarded with increased income. In fact, because profits are divided among the workforce, those who work hard may be subsidising shirkers.

Thirdly, employee ownership may undermine trade union strength and solidarity. If employee investment encourages workers to identify with capital, this may undercut the trade union's adversarial role as the employees' independent representatives in collective bargaining. Moreover, in employee buyout situations, tension may be created between local and national union officials. Anxious to secure jobs at a plant threatened with closure, the local union may agree to a wage reduction that undermines nationally negotiated rates. There is a risk that employee-owners will be hurt in the long run by such diminution of trade union influence.

In this chapter we examine the literature relating to the influence of organised labour, and other possible reasons why some employees invest while others do not.

The British labour movement and employee ownership

If local trade unions have workforce support, then their cooperation is likely to be necessary (though not sufficient) for a successful buyout (Stern and Hammer, 1978). However, trade unions have traditionally been opposed to employee ownership in all its forms. Workers' interests were believed to be best served through strong unions which could challenge employers' control. In this view industrial democracy would be furthered by trade union organisation in collective bargaining, ancillary trade union services and central planning through the collective ownership of the means of production (Webb, 1897). The producer cooperative movement would in contrast remain peripheral; such organisations would be ineffective islands in a sea of capitalism (Webb, 1921). Though they might obtain working capital from capitalist financiers, they would either remain small and eccentric, go bankrupt, or if successful convert to conventional forms of joint-stock ownership. Similarly, employee share ownership and profit-sharing schemes have not traditionally been part of the British labour movement's demands for greater industrial democracy.[1] Until recently, employee financial participation was of peripheral importance in the remuneration package offered in conventionally owned companies. The seminal work of Weitzman (1984) has increased attention to the potential of employee share ownership and flexible pay.

The trade unions' scepticism and hostility derived in part from the experience of early profit-sharing schemes. From the 1860s to the First World War, the introduction of such schemes appeared to coincide with periods of high labour unrest. They were overtly designed to detach workers from their trade unions, improve labour productivity and overcome resistance to change (Ramsay, 1977).[2] These schemes eschewed the philanthropic paternalism of Robert Owen, which had influenced the early producer cooperative movement, and were explicitly manipulative.

As the unions established themselves in many sectors, employee financial participation posed much less threat to their existence. Until recently, however, their resistance continued.[3] The schemes were seen as management strategies designed to co-opt workers or to contain employee discontent and conflict. Without giving employees control over managerial decisions, or significantly reducing the inequalities of wealth in society, ownership would undercut traditional trade union institutions dedicated to increasing the power of workers.

This view of employee ownership as a subtle form of management control tends to ignore the double-edged nature of such a strategy (Gamson, 1968; Lockett, 1981). Partial employee ownership may also improve labour's access to resources which could increase its influence and control over production.[4] Thus, managers too may also have reservations about a scheme which increases labour's influence at the expense of middle management. Each case must be evaluated individually to assess its net consequences for employees, weighing any increased managerial control over the workforce that results from employee ownership conversion against any increase in workers' control over decision-making.

Trade unions today must adjust to dramatically changing market and managerial environments. In particular, privatisation is fundamentally changing the nature of employee financial interests in Britain, extending those interests far beyond the simple wage packet upon which traditional trade unionism was based. This shift has been achieved by: (i) distributing shares to employees in privatisation (between 1979 and 1988, 700,000 new employee-shareholders were created in the course of 15 major privatisations); (ii) encouraging individual private investment in privatised enterprises and other quoted companies (in 1988 there were some 10 million shareholders in Britain, or about 19 per cent of the adult population, up from 7 per cent in 1979);[5] and (iii) the sale of council housing (this was the main form of privatisation during 1979–83 when nearly 600,000 units were sold; a further 300,000 were sold during 1984–6).

Employers in the private sector increasingly view employee share schemes as an important means of motivating the workforce. But most schemes introduced under the Finance Acts since 1978 have been non-negotiable. A Department of Employment survey (Smith, 1986) revealed that 60 per cent of firms with approved schemes recognise trade unions, but only some 20 per cent consulted the trade unions in the early stages. The trade unions did not object initially to this failure to consult them. Now, however, key trade unions, including the Electrical Electronic Telecommunication and Plumbing Union (EETPU) and the Banking Insurance and Finance Union (BIFU), have active policies on employee share schemes which are available to members (Incomes Data Services, 1986).[6] These unions are increasingly willing to cooperate if a plan is judged on a joint basis and if they are given greater access to company information on profits. Further, several trade unions support the Unity Trust Bank plc, and have helped it to promote its own brand of employee financial participation similar to the share-based scheme introduced under the Finance Act 1978. To date the bank has financed a half-dozen or so employee buyouts.

The local trade union may have the power to prevent a buyout. For example, the government's announcement of its intention to sell Yarrow Shipbuilders was followed by both an external bid and an attempted management-led buyout. Local union opposition eventually aborted the buyout attempt. On the other hand, some successful buyouts have been led by the local trade union officials, notably at Kirby Manufacturing and Engineering Company Ltd in Britain and Rath Packing Company in the United States (Bradley and Gelb, 1986).

Empirical evidence suggests that the trade union's influence will not necessarily decline after an employee buyout. Wright and Coyne's (1985) survey of British management buyouts showed that employees and trade unions are generally positive about the conversions. Employees and their representatives preferred to continue negotiating with managements they knew and could trust to keep the plants open, rather than face the uncertainty of a sale to outsiders. Only 10 per cent of the surveyed buyouts involved share participation by non-managerial employees, so there was little threat to the unions as stakeholders in collective bargaining. In a case study of Panache Upholstery, where employees invested their redundancy payments in a management-led buyout in 1980, the union did not resist the new organisation.[7] If employee investment was necessary, it argued, a producer cooperative which eroded some managerial prerogatives and increased the voice of ordinary workers was preferable to a management buyout which retained a conventional corporate structure.

Hypotheses about decisions to invest

Employees' investment decisions will depend on the circumstances surrounding the introduction of an employee financial participation scheme or a conversion to employee ownership. For example, only ideological diehards are likely to resist an offer of free shares. When British Telecom was privatised, some 96 per cent of eligible employees accepted the opportunity to acquire 54 free shares with an initial value of some £75 (Newman, 1986).[8] Similarly, in the approved profit-sharing schemes, employees make no investment. Shares are allocated to employees unless they decline the offer. In the savings-related share option schemes, there is no obligation to take up an option following the termination of the Save-As-You-Earn (SAYE) contract, and the employee's decision is likely to depend upon the capital gains to be made. Why the employee first decides to enter a contract is a more complex question.

Because employee buyouts have traditionally been organised to avert plant closures, employees may invest in their company in order to preserve their jobs. They may channel their savings, as well as any redundancy payments if there has been a break in employment, into a new enterprise in order to secure a longer-term income stream from employment.[9] Sometimes manning cuts and cost reductions are crucial to securing viability in the new enterprise. At Scottish News Enterprises, for example, only 25 per cent of the previous workforce was re-employed (Bradley and Gelb, 1983a). In most cases, a self-selection process occurs during the transition period, so that those who invest are those most in need of their existing jobs.

At Scottish News Enterprises a second screening process effectively eliminated a group termed fatalists by Bradley and Gelb (1983a): workers who did not think that the plant could be saved by their own efforts. All in all, then, if dramatic changes are required to secure the continuation of a plant, the employees who remain will tend to have poor alternative prospects but believe that their increased effort could potentially save the enterprise.[10]

Although Bradley and Gelb's (1983a) hypothesis dealt with corporate divestitures of moderately profitable plants, it is perhaps best suited to explain the employee investment decision when plant closures or redundancies are imminent. If bids from management-led consortia occur, allowing employees to exercise a freer choice, an alternative approach may be required to explain the investment decision. If a subsidiary is potentially profitable, then employees may be willing to assume major risk in return for independence and the incentives of ownership, particularly if the sale price represents a discount on asset value. Between 1979 and 1983, in the West Midlands engineering sector, the discount on asset value in management buyouts averaged 45 per cent, but varied from case to case according to the relative bargaining strength of the vendors and buyout team (Wright and Coyne, 1985: p. 6).[11] Furthermore, the financial institutions may look to management's willingness to provide at least some equity capital as an important indicator of their commitment to the success of a buyout. In some cases, therefore, the investment decision may reflect a need to show confidence in management and the workforce, and to demonstrate leadership.

Some potentially profitable units have been sold to workforces, rather than to the managers alone. The main examples are from North America where corporate divestitures of moderately profitable medium-sized enterprises have included Vermont Asbestos Group, Saratoga Knitting Mill, South Bend Lathe Inc. and Byers Transport Limited.[12] Employee participation has typically been far from universal. For example, at Saratoga

Knitting Mill 70 per cent of the new firm's shares were held by only 30 per cent of employees. At Byers Transport Limited only 70 per cent of employees participated in ownership of 100 per cent of the shares. At a library furniture manufacturer in Herkimer, New York, which was closed in 1976 and bought by employees and the local community, some 35 per cent of the equity was held by workers, but only 36 per cent of them participated (Stern et al., 1979). The pattern of employee investment at the National Freight Company is similar. At the time of the buyout, 40 per cent of the NFC's workforce bought 82.5 per cent of the equity, and since then another 25 per cent of the workforce have become employee-shareholders.

To date, no satisfactory explanation of the decision pattern has been advanced. For example, the employee's decision may depend on his ability to afford an investment. Those with a low disposable income may choose not to save and therefore may be unable to invest. However, in most recorded buyouts, favourable loans were provided to support employee investments. Another possibility is that employees who joined the firm after the conversion did not feel it exigent to invest or were not invited to do so. There may be some substance in this explanation, particularly if the new enterprise appears to be succeeding. But it cannot explain why some of those who were employed at the firm before the conversion declined to invest although they could afford to do so.

Here we explore two contrasting hypotheses about an employee's investment decision when a public sector enterprise is converted to majority employee ownership under a corporate model were individual holdings are permitted. This was the case at NFC. One possibility is that investment is undertaken as a defensive action to prevent job loss. Alternatively, employees may invest in their company for financial gain. Each hypothesis suggests reasons why some employees invest and others do not.

Dependence hypothesis

The predominantly American phenomenon of concession bargaining, in which employees can negotiate a wage cut in return for a share in the equity of their firm has been viewed as a way of rescuing troubled companies (see, for example, *Industrial Relations Review and Report*, 1984). Similarly in a buyout situation, from either the public or private sector, employees may fear a sale to a third party, which might attempt to renationalise operations or reduce the firms' assets, thereby creating job losses. A buyout may therefore be understood as a defensive measure to prevent redundancies, and the employee investment decision as the acceptance of income risk in order to reduce employment risk.

Under this hypothesis, the utility-maximising employee will invest in a buyout if the expected benefits of doing so exceed those of looking for another job. The expected duration of unemployment, the nature of the anticipated job and the level of wages expected elsewhere must all be considered. Employees will differ in their analysis of this choice problem, and the most pessimistic will be those who feel they have few or no alternative job opportunities, or could not obtain a job with comparable benefits. The local unemployment rate, occupational unemployment rate, individual skills, work experience, and so on, will influence the individual's dependence upon employment at the existing firm.

Dependence may also vary along the course of the life cycle. Employees with family responsibilities may be less mobile and more willing to protect their jobs by investing in an employee buyout. Homeowners with high current expenses may also fear income insecurity and choose to invest rather than to risk job search. Regional variations in house prices may be a further constraint upon employee mobility. Alternatively, individuals very close to retirement may feel less dependent, and more willing to be made redundant. Employees most dependent on the firm will be most concerned about its survival and profitability. They may be prepared to invest in maintaining a plant or firm to protect their own jobs. Such employees could form the core of a buyout team.

The validity of the dependence hypothesis may depend on the context of the change in ownership, and particularly on whether it is prompted by a crisis at the firm. Employees' anxiety would be most acute if redundancies or closure seemed imminent. Otherwise they might not even recognise their dependence. In a non-crisis situation, moreover, the effect of life-cycle factors is not clear. If the employee recognises that family responsibilities increase his dependence, he may decide to invest. But his personal commitments may also make him exceptionally risk-averse. If so, and if investment is not dictated by a crisis situation, he may choose not to participate. Thus, life-cycle factors may cut either way.

Information hypothesis

If employees invest primarily as a means of seeking financial gains, their decision will depend upon the information and advice available on the company's future profitability. On this basis, they will assess the risks of investment and the opportunity costs that influence their eventual decision.

Under this hypothesis the utility-maximising investor will invest in his firm only if he expects to achieve a better return than he could by investing elsewhere. His position as an employee within the organisation may give him informational advantages that outweigh the risks of concentrating assets.[13] However, the information and advice available is likely to vary considerably among groups of employees. The main source of such informational asymmetry may be occupation. Because of their functional responsibilities, some occupational groups will have access to more information. Management might reasonably be assumed to have the greatest access to the financial information needed to make objective decisions about the company's overall performance and potential profitability. Firms may attempt to distribute information to other occupational groups through communications and joint consultation networks, but are unlikely to share sensitive information concerning product development, future investment and other information relevant to investment decision. Non-managerial employees may therefore have to seek information and advice elsewhere, although clerical employees in small profit centres may informally receive the benefits of management's superior information.

Manual employees are the occupational group least likely to receive company financial information. Their functional duties normally restrict their sphere of control and allow little access to detailed company information.[14] In addition, informally received information may be difficult to evaluate in low-trust environments. However, trade unions may represent an alternative source of information for these employees, quite possibly their dominant source of information in a preconversion situation.

A trade union may oppose a buyout for at least four reasons. Firstly, it concentrates their members' economic risk. Secondly, employee ownership may be perceived to threaten the unions' traditional collective bargaining role. Share ownership may blur the differences of interests between the individual employee and the company and consequently may highlight the differences between the individual's interests and the trade union's interests as represented by collective bargaining strength. Thirdly, during a transition to employee ownership a local union may agree to a wage cut in order to secure a conversion. This may undermine nationally negotiated wage rates and lead to conflict between local and national union officials. Fourthly, employee equity participation need not mean increased participation in decision-making or increased employee voice. Employees may make concessions without gaining any greater control over the company policy. If so, employee ownership might work against the achievement of greater industrial democracy.

A trade union's influence among manual employees may be greater in some parts of the firm than others. In smaller centres where unions tend to be less powerful or active (as such centres represent high cost/low return activity), management's influence may be stronger and formal information may be more freely extended to manual employees. Furthermore, in this higher-trust environment, informal information may be received more willingly. External sources of advice such as the press, family and associates may further reduce trade union influence and other forms of informational asymmetry. For example, homeowners have a perspective that may help them address the investment decision:

> Owner occupiers become embroiled in the worlds of property and capital . . . They watch interest rates, worry about property values . . . Individual households are minor property owners, connected directly to the institutions of big finance capitalism . . . All this integrates them into the network of banks, building societies, finance houses and rich private investors. (Mann, 1985: p. 12)

Thus, some manual employees in strong trade union sections may well depart from union policy.

5

The employee investment decision at the NFC

Introduction

Little research has yet been devoted to the question of why employees choose to invest in buyout situations. For some time it was assumed that risk-averse employees would not be predisposed to invest in the place where they worked (Samuelson, 1977). In the case of the NFC, however, large numbers of employees did invest. In February 1982, at the first investment opportunity, some 40 per cent of the NFC workforce bought a tranche of shares and by March 1986 the figure had increased to over 60 per cent.

Chapter 4 developed two hypotheses to explain this phenomenon: the dependence and informational asymmetry hypotheses. Here we test those hypotheses empirically. Findings are based on some 60 in-depth interviews with senior management, employees and trade union officials in the NFC; questionnaire survey data from an NFC subsidiary: BRS (Southern); and company data.[1] We shall first present the analysis from the non-questionnaire survey data, then look closely at the specific hypotheses in the questionnaire data.[2] Interviewees gave some support to both hypotheses. Overall, however, the balance of evidence (and particularly the questionnaire survey) favours the informational asymmetry hypothesis.

Qualitative findings

Interviewees mentioned the context in which the privatisation of the NFC took place, namely the economic recession of the early 1980s and fears of fragmentation of the organisation. Senior management at the NFC in particular were keen to emphasise the defensive nature of the buyout. According to a senior manager:

> Our main fear was that the NFC would be taken over by asset-strippers. This would undoubtedly have shaken out many

jobs at the operations level. On top of that, we were afraid that breaking up the organisation would have meant that some of our managers would not be required in the organisations of the buying companies. The fear of job loss therefore covered our entire organisation.

The implication was that investment was primarily determined by dependence on the firm.

However, the fear of job loss was probably less widespread than this comment suggests. Fragmenting the NFC would undoubtedly have affected employment in each occupational group, but the most vulnerable employees would probably have been the central, non-operational staff and those in poorly performing profit centres. These categories included Head Office personnel and employees in the loss-making parcels activities of National Carriers and Roadline. Circumstances were somewhat different in most of the NFC's other operations. For example, at the research site, BRS (Southern), there did not appear to be a general feeling of contraction or closure. Furthermore, between 1979 and 1984 the unemployment rates in south-east England were consistently some 2 or 3 per cent lower than the British national average. In the areas surrounding the depots surveyed, unemployment rates were close to the regional averages. Clearly unemployment pressures and fears of job loss were distinctly lower in the case study subsidiary than in some other sections of the NFC.

Interviews with branch managers at BRS (Southern) suggested less concern about the job protection role of the buyout than existed at the corporate level. BRS (Southern) managers' decisions to invest had been determined primarily by expectations of capital gains. One branch manager suggested that 'there was a good case for a quick buck. Anyone who took shares was looking for a quick buck and a stable old age. To a lot of managers it was obvious that the shares had to go up in the first place because of the amount of assets we were buying.' This view was supported by another manager from the same branch: 'financially, I couldn't see the buyout losing. The price that the shares were offered at was very good, and I believed that the NFC did a very good job.' The managers believed others at their depot had invested for similar reasons, although some employees might have invested under the misguided impression that they were 'buying their jobs'. When asked why all employees had not taken advantages of the opportunity, branch managers suggested several reasons. For example, they felt that some employees did not think they could afford to invest ('although I can't understand why everyone did not take the loan'). Other managers referred to the ignorance of shareholding among many employees, and the perception of older employees who had known BRS during bad times. The union view was seen as very influential.

Managers believed that many workers had followed the union line, although, as one branch manager remarked, 'I'm sure they're kicking themselves now.' Much seems to have depended on the position taken by the local shop steward, which varied from depot to depot. Another depot manager suggested: 'One of the main reasons why drivers didn't buy was because the T and G [Transport and General Workers' Union] were against it and the shop steward at our branch followed what the union said and advised people not to buy shares.'

Further interviews with employees at BRS (Southern) yielded less conclusive data. Interviewees were disaggregated into three broad occupational groups. Fifteen were supervisors or foremen, 13 were clerical employees and the remaining 25 were blue-collar employees. Interviewees were asked why they had or had not invested in the NFC. Typically, multiple reasons were cited, straddling the two hypotheses. This finding suggested, as had been suspected, that the two hypotheses were not mutually exclusive. Among those who did invest, many gave more than one reason. Sixty-three per cent said they had seen share purchase as a 'good investment'. Forty-three per cent said they feared fragmentation if the company went to outsiders and therefore invested to protect their jobs. Some 26 per cent invested to create an 'identity with the company' which suggested that an attraction of the buyout may have been a feeling of self-employment. Responses suggested that employees saw job security as closely related to the company's success. According to a manual employee-shareholder: 'I wanted the company to succeed. It's your job and if the company fails you lose your job.' Similarly, a white-collar employee-shareholder said: 'I thought it was a good idea at the time. We were frightened of asset-strippers and jobs going and we were advised that it would be a good investment which gave another incentive.' Those who did not invest cited three main reasons, which were often mutually reinforcing. Forty-six per cent said that they could not afford to invest. Forty-five per cent were unconvinced that an investment in the NFC was financially sound. Only 21 per cent mentioned the advice of the trade union or any sort of ideological opposition to privatisation.

The ability of employees to afford an investment is a vexed question. This issue was clearly of importance to many non-managerial employees. A clerical employee stated: 'At the time [of the buyout] I was saving money for the home. I couldn't afford to buy shares, especially only two months after Christmas.' Another employee indicated that he was able to invest because he could afford to: 'I bought £200 of shares. I took a risk with money I would not miss.'

The question of 'affording to buy' is closely linked with access to information about the company's future prospects. To facilitate purchase,

73

a £200 interest-free loan was made available to all employees at the time of the buyout. Moreover, a loan on the same terms has been available periodically during wider share ownership campaigns to new employees and existing employees who wished to purchase shares for the first time. Therefore, an employee's statement that he could not afford to invest suggests that either the benefits of the loan were unclear, high financial responsibilities had made the employee unusually risk-averse, or he lacked good information on the company's prospects.

The main indication that many non-investors were misinformed emerged from those respondents who did not consider the NFC to be a good investment. As the hypothesis predicts, these were mainly manual employees. The comments of two drivers are illustrative: 'Having been here thirty years, I'm not impressed with the company's record.' 'At the time, company couldn't give good wage rises, so why buy shares.' The TGWU's recommendation was also mentioned as a source of counteracting information. It was not universally heeded, however. A clerical employee remarked that 'the union's influence was not important here. Personal opinions were more important.' Another clerical worker noted: 'I did hear that the trade unions said don't buy. But they never said that to me personally.' This comment also indicated that clerical employees may have been unaware of the differences in the positions of the several trade unions.

Taken as a whole, the interviews suggest that an employee's investment decision depended on various mutually reinforcing factors. It is not possible to estimate which reasons were most important. The quantitative evidence from the questionnaire survey is more conclusive.

Questionnaire survey findings

The dependence and informational asymmetry hypotheses were examined more formally in the questionnaire survey. Each hypothesis generates its own set of propositions concerning the investment decision of employees and the characteristics of employee-shareholders. These propositions and the findings are now investigated more closely.

Dependence hypothesis

Employee investment is a defensive measure taken by desperate workers with low expectations of alternative employment opportunities and/or high financial responsibilities. Specific propositions follow:

Proposition 1: *Age and dependence*
Older employees are more likely to invest.

Proposition 2: *Individual skills*

The lower the individual's skill level and breadth of work experience, the higher the likelihood of investment.

Proposition 3: *Life-cycle factors*

Life-cycle factors compound dependence, leading to a greater propensity to invest. Therefore (i) those with family responsibilities are more likely to invest than those without such responsibilities, and (ii) those with high current housing expenses are more likely to invest than those without such expenses.

Proposition 1: Age and dependence

Previous empirical research has indicated a significant correlation between age and downgrading following re-employment after unemployment. MacKay and Reid (1972) found age to be the most important variable influencing the length of unemployment post-redundancy. Workers older than 55 had particular difficulty in finding re-employment. Earlier studies had also shown the older worker's difficulty in seeking re-employment following redundancy. In a national survey of the unemployed, Daniel (1974) found that older redundant workers had greater difficulty in finding any re-employment, and the jobs they eventually found were a downgrading on their previous jobs. Further, older workers were more likely to drop out of the labour market altogether. Nickell (1979 and 1980) confirmed previous findings that the number of spells of unemployment for those aged under 20 was high, but the duration of each spell was short. As age increased the number of spells decreased, reaching a minimum between the ages of 40 and 54, but the average duration increased steadily with age. Bradley and Gelb (1983a) found that those who self-selected themselves to participate in the employee buyout at Scottish News Enterprises in 1974 tended to be older workers. Eighty-five per cent of their respondents had been unemployed for at least a year before the 'Scottish Daily News' was launched; 74 per cent of the group were 44 or older.

The questionnaire survey investigated this issue at the NFC. Twenty-six per cent of the sample were aged over 51 and 47 per cent were aged between 31 and 50. Forty-five per cent of the sample were employee-share-holders and 55 per cent were non-shareholders. The dependence hypothesis suggests that the older workers will be more likely to invest, but data do not confirm this prediction. Overall, 51 per cent of those aged over 51 invested, compared with 41 per cent of those aged 31 to 50 and approximately 46 per cent of those aged 30 or under. But it is more meaningful to examine a sub-sample consisting of those who had joined the NFC before the buyout and therefore were more likely to perceive a threat of

Table 5.1. *Relationship between employee ownership and age[a]*

	Shareholders %	Non-Shareholders %	Sample %
Age			
16–30	70.0	30.0	17.9 (n = 20)
31–40	45.7	54.3	31.3 (n = 35)
41–50	38.1	61.9	18.8 (n = 21)
51 +	52.8	47.2	32.0 (n = 36)
Total	50.9	49.1	100.0 (n = 112)

Chi-square = 4.725, not significant at 0.193 with 3 degrees of freedom.

*[a] Pre-buyout sub-sample.

unemployment. Of this sub-group some 51 per cent were employee shareholders and 49 per cent were non-shareholders. Although the youngest and oldest employees had the highest propensity to invest, differences were not statistically significant (see Table 5.1).

Proposition 2: Individual skills

Nickell (1979 and 1980) showed that the duration of unemployment does not vary greatly according to skill levels, but the probability of entering unemployment is higher with lower levels of skill. The second proposition, therefore, suggests than the least skilled employees will bear the highest risks from threatened job losses, making them more likely to invest. The survey investigated this issue in a number of ways. Firstly, the manual workforce was divided into three skill categories. Engineers and fitters were classified as skilled, drivers as semi-skilled, and warehousemen and cleaners as unskilled. These groups' propensities to become employee-shareholders were then compared for the sub-sample who joined the NFC before the buyout. Some 40 per cent of skilled workers, 31.5 per cent of semi-skilled and 40 per cent of unskilled workers invested, which suggests that individual skills were not significant.

Statistically significant relationships did emerge, however, when blue-collar and white-collar employees, and management and non-management employees were compared (Table 5.2). The greater propensity of white-collar and managerial employees to invest can probably be explained better by the informational asymmetry hypothesis than by a skill factor. The main skill factor, for example, within the blue-collar workforce, showed no significant associations.

Additional variables were considered to measure an employee's skill

Table 5.2. *Relationship between employee ownership and occupational group[a]*

	Blue-collar %	White-Collar %	Total %
Employee ownership			
Shareholders	33.8	77.3	50.9
Non-shareholders	66.2	22.7	49.1
% of sample	60.7	39.3	100.0
	(n = 68)	(n = 44)	(n = 112)

Chi-square = 20.179, significant at 0.001 with 1 degree of freedom.

	Non-managers %	Managers %	Total %
Employee ownership			
Shareholders	41.0	79.3	50.9
Non-shareholders	59.0	20.7	49.1
% of sample	74.1	25.9	100.0
	(n = 83)	(n = 29)	(n = 112)

Chi-square = 12.645, significant at 0.001, with 1 degree of freedom.

[a] Pre-buyout sub-sample.

factor if seeking re-employment. It seems likely that the longer one stays with the same firm, the more job-specific or firm-specific one's skills become. Long duration of employment may therefore give an employee the opportunity to acquire increased human capital, which may enhance productivity. But long duration may prove dysfunctional when seeking re-employment, particularly if one's work history has not included experience with many firms previously. A prospective employer may consider retraining of such recruits cost-inefficient.

Data on employees' length of service presented ambiguous results. No linear relationship emerged with share ownership. Thirty per cent of those who joined the firm after the buyout, between February 1982 and September 1984, were shareholders, compared with 51 per cent of those who joined before the buyout. The low level of share participation among new recruits may be explained by the high labour turnover rate in the company for new employees, and a lower awareness of the buyout and its history. Also, the intensity of the consortium's efforts to communicate information about employee ownership and share purchase may have decreased after the buyout. This was suggested in interview responses of some new recruits. One young clerical employee who joined in November 1982 said, 'I was asked if I wanted to buy shares. I considered it, but did not know

Table 5.3. *Number of previous companies by employee ownership*[a]

	No previous employer %	1–2 employers %	3 + previous employers %	Total %
Employee ownership				
Shareholders	83.3	45.2	44.2	50.9
Non-shareholders	16.7	54.8	55.8	49.1
% of sample	16.1	37.5	46.4	100.0
	(n = 18)	(n = 42)	(n = 52)	(n = 112)

Chi-square = 9.040, significant at 0.05 with 2 degrees of freedom.

[a] Pre-buyout sub-sample.

enough about it.' Another employee who joined a month earlier said, 'I was interested in shares, but they didn't send me a brochure.'

A low dependence on the company may help explain why post-buyout recruits were less likely to invest, but is unlikely to be the dominant influence. The highest propensity to invest (60 per cent) was found among those who had been with the company over 25 years; but they formed less than 10 per cent of the sample. The chi-square test proved statistically insignificant with four degrees of freedom.

A tenuous relationship appeared to exist between share ownership and an employee's previous movements in the labour market, as measured by the number of companies he had previously worked at (Table 5.3). The dependence hypothesis predicts that those with less previous experience are more likely to feel dependent on the firm, and consequently to invest. Some 88 per cent of employees with no previous experience invested, although only 16 per cent of the total sample were included in this sub-sample. The proportion of shareholders was much lower in groups with prior employment history. The differences were marginally significant at 0.05.

Proposition 3: Life-cycle factors

The third proposition suggests that certain life-cycle factors may increase an employee's need for security of disposable income. This effect may compound an employee's dependence on the firm, making him invest. The relevant factors relate specifically to familial and financial responsibilities. A family may be less willing than an individual to move in the labour market in order to find re-employment. An employee who is an owner-occupier is probably especially reluctant to move.

The evidence suggests that life-cycle factors do not affect employees' natural risk-aversion in the hypothesised way. In fact, heavy responsibilities may make employees feel they cannot afford to invest. One respondent commented 'I didn't believe in a buyout. Anyway, I've got my mortgage to pay off.' Employees who joined the company before the buyout were asked whether they were married and/or had young children. No significant relationship appeared to exist between share ownership and marital status. A statistically significant relationship ($p < 0.01$) did emerge between share ownership and responsibility for children, but not in the expected direction. Seventy-one per cent of those with no responsibility for children invested compared to only 42 per cent of those with children, suggesting that children may constitute an income drain that makes employees more risk-averse rather than more willing to invest. Home ownership had no statistically significant relationship with share ownership in the pre-buyout sub-sample, although 53 per cent of homeowners invested compared with 39 per cent of tenants in private-rented or council accommodation.

Informational asymmetry hypothesis

Events at the NFC and the BRS (Southern) before and after the buyout suggest that the informational asymmetry hypothesis may be more predictive than the dependence hypothesis. Senior managers at NFC were confidentially consulted in the early stages of the buyout about its prospects and the level of support it would receive. Furthermore, when the decision to proceed with buyout was formally made, the NFC's 2,300 managers were briefed in a series of presentations during which they were informed about NFC's potential profitability. Questionnaires were distributed at these meetings asking whether managers would make investments, which received very positive responses. The majority of the workforce did not participate in this early process. Company information concerning a staff buyout and its prospects was first presented during August 1981 at a series of short video presentations at local promotion meetings attended by the Organising Committee and other senior managers to encourage employee investment. The details were elaborated in the Prospectus issued in January 1982, inviting employees to buy shares, and in a second video and local communications campaign including free phone-ins.

Trade union organisation at the NFC was strong and influential, although the extent of its influence varied between unions and locations. Union activity appeared to be dominated by the Transport and General Workers Union (TGWU), who represented some 85 per cent of manual employees as well as some lower supervisory grades, and was particularly powerful in the larger urban depots. Manual employees received strong guidelines from this union, which appeared to be a major source of informational asymmetry. Company sources were in favour of the buyout and their highly professional communications campaign encouraged investment. On the other hand, the trade unions' position was ambivalent. After initial opposition to any privatisation of the NFC, and scepticism about the viability of an employee buyout, the Transport Salaried Staff Association (TSSA), which represented clerical employees, the National Union of Railwaymen (NUR) and the Amalgamated Union of Engineering Workers (AUEW) all accepted an employee buyout as the most acceptable privatisation option. The smallest union, the United Road Transport Union (URTU), was the most positive and enthusiastic about the possibility of employee ownership and gave its full support. However, the key union, the TGWU, took a different position.

At the end of June 1981, Mr A. Kitson, the TGWU's Deputy General Secretary, made consensual approaches to the consortium. He said that if the NFC had to be sold then it should be sold as one unit. This was an informal endorsement of the buyout. Kitson called for consultation with the consortium before the TGWU took a formal position.

Interviews with regional TGWU officials at the NFC suggest that greater trade union support for the proposals could have been mobilised if the consortium had been willing to form a producer cooperative. Thomas (1984) suggests that the trade unions at the NFC might have been able to resist the sale, or at least to force concessions: 'City and management opinion was very nervous about the novelty of the NFC buyout and the impact of the recession. Well-timed industrial disruption might have sunk the flotation.' (Thomas, 1984: p. 64). An alternative view is that the trade unions' lack of activity and the eventual positions they took demonstrate their relative weakness during this period. The NUR, TSSA and AUEW eventually concluded that given the government's commitment to privatising the NFC, a buyout which enabled a high level of employee share participation was the most acceptable option. But the TGWU, which had initially taken this more conciliatory view, hardened its position. In July, Kitson rejected the buyout option and announced the TGWU's opposition to privatisation:

> In the TGWU's view share purchases for the workers are aimed at undermining opposition to the asset-stripping of the public sector . . . The shares likely to be on offer are going to be cheques that can only be cashed by redundancies . . . In effect, the worker shareholders would have no real control. They would be a conscripted group with no option but to pass their own death sentences when the NFC is further asset stripped . . . worker shares arising in this sort of situation, under this Government are a meal ticket to the dole queue. (see McLachlan, 1983: p. 64).

Committed to renationalisation on the return of a Labour government, the TGWU recommended that its members not join the consortium. This was viewed as the best way of resisting the buyout.

Company sources suggest that the TGWU's policy recommendation had most impact in south-east England. At the subsidiary BRS (Southern), for example, the low take-up of shares, initially only some 20 per cent of the workforce, may be explained by the TGWU's traditional strength in this company, particularly in the depots in the London area.

Information concerning the potential for capital gains was either not fully available to manual employees, or was counteracted by the TGWU's advice in an environment where management was often viewed with suspicion. The variability of the trade union's influence across depots is seen in the figures on share purchase. At BRS (Southern)'s largest depot where the union is considered to be strongest and the most militant, only an estimated 4 per cent of employees were shareholders at the time of the study, whereas at one of the smallest depots, some 80 per cent of employees had invested.

The questionnaire survey made a closer examination of the informational asymmetry hypothesis. Specific propositions were tested:

Proposition 1: *Employee share ownership*
Managers have the highest propensity to become shareholders and manual employees the lowest.
Proposition 2: *Trade union membership*
(i) Members of the TGWU are less likely to invest than other trade unionists, and (ii) members of the TGWU are less likely to invest than the rest of the workforce.
Proposition 3: *Locational effects*
The propensity to invest is higher at the smaller depots than at the larger depots.
Proposition 4: *External factors*
The propensity to invest varies according to employees' access to external sources of information, such as education and financial institutions.

Proposition 1: Employee share ownership by occupation

Table 5.4 examines the proposition regarding occupation. Over 71 per cent

Table 5.4. *Relationship between employee ownership and occupation*

	Management %	Clerical %	Manual %	Total %
Employee ownership				
Shareholders	71.1	65.2	29.7	45.4
Non-shareholders	28.9	34.8	70.3	54.6
% of sample	25.0	15.1	59.9	100.0
	(n = 38)	(n = 23)	(n = 91)	(n = 152)

Chi-square = 22.815, significant at 0.001 with 2 degrees of freedom.

The employee investment decision at the NFC

Table 5.5. *Internal labour market and employee ownership*

	Promoted %	Same job %	Not promoted %	Total %
Employee ownership				
Shareholders	61.5	42.9	31.0	45.4
Non-shareholders	38.5	57.1	69.0	54.6
% of sample	25.6	55.3	19.1	100.0
	(n = 39)	(n = 84)	(n = 29)	(n = 152)

Chi-square = 6.731, significant at 0.05 with 2 degrees of freedom.

of managers in the sample became shareholders, as did some 65 per cent of clerical employees. But only about 30 per cent of manual employees became shareholders. The differences are statistically significant at the 0.001 level with two degrees of freedom suggesting a strong association between employee share ownership and occupation. The interest-free loan available from the NFC should have facilitated investment by lower-paid employees.

Supplementary data also supports the occupational proposition. Those who have benefited from the firm's internal labour market and were promoted during their period of service had access to more company information than was previously available to them. The hypothesis predicts that such employees would be more likely to invest than the rest of the workforce. Table 5.5 shows this to be so. Some 62 per cent of employees who had been promoted in the company were shareholders and the chi-square test with two degrees of freedom was statistically significant at the 0.05 level. However, only some 26 per cent of the sample were in this sub-group.

Proposition 2: Trade union membership

Trade union affiliation in the questionnaire survey divided as follows: 61 per cent were members of the TGWU; 17 per cent belonged to other unions; and 22 per cent were not trade union members. The first step was to measure employee share ownership in relation to trade union membership regardless of union affiliation. Share ownership was more common among non-trade unionists, 58 per cent of whom invested, compared with 42 per cent of trade union members. The difference did not represent a statistically significant relationship, however. The chi-square was very low with one degree of freedom, and significance was only achieved to 0.112.

For several reasons, it seemed that this overall picture might be misleading. Firstly, trade union members included some management and clerical employees who had alternative sources of information within the firm. Secondly, because the company was a post-entry closed shop for manual grades, union membership may not always have been desired, reducing the influence of any trade union advice. Thirdly, the advice of the unions differed. Only the TGWU maintained opposition to the buyout and advised members accordingly. Hence the second proposition is divided into two sub-propositions:

(i) *Members of the TGWU are less likely to invest than other trade unionists.*

Support for the proposition would be unsurprising, given the substantial coincidence between membership of the TGWU and BRS (Southern)'s manual employees, but countervailing forces also exist, namely the closed shop and the inclusion of supervisory grades in the TGWU. In fact TGWU members were much less likely to invest than the other trade union members in the sample (Table 5.6). Thirty-four per cent of TGWU members were shareholders compared with 69 per cent of members of the other trade unions. The difference was significant in the chi-square test with one degree of freedom.

(ii) *Members of the TGWU are less likely to invest than the rest of the sample.*

TGWU members were also considerably less likely to invest than the rest of the sample, including non-trade unionists (Table 5.7). The chi-square test was statistically significant to 0.001 with one degree of freedom.

Proposition 3: The effects of location

Despite the strong influence of the TGWU's advice, some 31 per cent of

Table 5.6. *Relationship between trade union membership and employee ownership*

	TGWU %	Others %	Total %
Employee ownership			
Shareholders	34.4	69.2	42.0
Non-shareholders	65.6	30.8	58.0
% of sample	78.2	21.8	100.0
	(n = 93)	(n = 26)	(n = 119)

Chi-square = 10.113, significant at 0.001 with 1 degree of freedom.

Table 5.7. *Relationship between membership of TGWU and employee ownership*

	Yes %	No %	Total %
Employee ownership			
Shareholders	34.4	62.7	45.4
Non-shareholders	65.6	37.3	54.6
% of sample	60.1	39.9	100.0
	(n = 93)	(n = 59)	(n = 152)

Chi-square = 11.666, significant at 0.001 with 1 degree of freedom.

manual employees in the sample did invest in the NFC. Only a few of these workers were members of other trade unions. This result reflects a diminution of the union's influence in small work sites.

Labour relations and conditions of employment in public sector road haulage were formalised considerably after nationalisation in 1947 (Bullock, 1960; Hollowell, 1968). It is not clear that this change made industrial relations more harmonious. Hollowell (1968) argued that the bureaucratic managerial system at BRS caused lower levels of job and work satisfaction among BRS' long distance (general haulage) drivers than among long distance drivers at private hauliers. He placed his discussion in the context of the interaction between the socio-technical system of traditional road haulage and the lorry driver's work ethos. Lorry driving, particularly over long distances, gives the driver a high level of independence, responsibility and discretion. It is an open socio-technical system that attracts highly individualistic and independent employees who enjoy the freedom from conventional supervision. Managements traditionally appreciated the discretion drivers had, and attempted to develop close, informal and high-trust relationships with them, which the drivers came to expect. Since road haulage was organised in small units it was feasible for a manager/owner to have such a relationship with all his employees. Furthermore, as it takes few vehicles to start one's own haulage activities, it was part of the driver's ethos to consider starting his own firm in the future. Hollowell (1968) suggested that this background was unlikely to be a good environment for either unionisation or high regulation.

Hollowell (1968) conducted open-ended interviews with BRS and non-BRS drivers; he found a major complaint of the BRS drivers was that the company's developed managerial system and hierarchy made managers unapproachable and that the high level of regulation reduced individuality. Frustration arose from the contradiction between a high level of

Table 5.8. *Relationship between employee ownership and depot size*

	Small %	Depot size Medium %	Large %	Total %
Employee ownership				
Shareholders	67.9	46.9	27.8	46.2
Non-shareholders	32.1	53.1	72.2	53.8
% of sample	18.7	56.3	25.0	100.0
	(n = 28)	(n = 81)	(n = 36)	(n = 145)

Chi-square = 10.215, significant at 0.05 with 2 degrees of freedom.

	Small %	Depot size Medium %	Large %	Total %
Manual employee ownership				
Shareholders	50.0	34.0	12.5	30.3
Non-shareholders	50.0	66.0	87.5	69.7
% of sample	13.3	60.1	26.6	100.0
	(n = 12)	(n = 53)	(n = 24)	(n = 89)

Chi-square = 6.138, significant at 0.05 with 2 degrees of freedom.

regulation, and an open socio-technical system which encouraged individuality and close relationships with managers. 'The existence of rules at BRS is the most striking difference between the two firms ... [the] BRS driver is given his job by clerical workers who hand out envelopes ... it is this part of the structure which articulates the conflict between mechanistic organisation and workers in open socio-technical systems' (Hollowell, 1968: p. 135). BRS drivers were seen as having less job and work satisfaction than drivers in private hauliers. Hollowell (1968) also interviewed employees in a textiles factory which had both a hierarchical managerial structure, and a closed socio-technical system. His conclusion was that 'the mechanistic nature of BRS produces a view of management which is at about the same level of favourability as that in the factory in spite of the presence of the lorry-driving socio-technical system at BRS' (Hollowell, 1968: p. 131).

It is perhaps prudent to treat these findings with caution as they were based on small samples using solely qualitative data. Nevertheless, it remains theoretically plausible that the impersonal nature of the mechanistic organisation at some BRS depots created labour tensions. Hollowell did not attempt to investigate whether the same characteristics were typical of the BRS network overall. This question is taken up more formally in this study.

It appears that there may be a relationship between the size of depot and the level of trade union activity. Hollowell's approach suggests a possible explanation. Perhaps in small BRS depots rule enforcement was high, but employees had personal contact with managers, which reduced the trade union's influence. But at the large depots, particularly in the London area, informal relations were not organisationally practical; as a result, the traditional orientations of the workforce gradually eroded and were replaced by positive attitudes towards trade unionism, fears of non-union external labour and eventually demands for the closed shop. If so, it would be wrong to conclude that the institutionalisation of labour relations created a universal change. Trade union strength was concentrated in the very large urban depots, particularly in the south-east.

Our data shows a clear, statistically significant relationship between location size and employee share ownership. When the company's depots are classified into three size categories (and the Head Office respondents are excluded), share ownership is seen to be much more common in the smaller than in the larger depots (Table 5.8). To correct for any distorting influence exerted by management and clerical employees in the sample, these employees were then excluded. Even among manual employees, the relationship between share ownership and branch is sustained, as shown in Table 5.8. This suggests that the variance in the level of union activity between depots may to some extent explain the pattern of manual employee investment.

Proposition 4: External factors

Alternatively, the variance in manual employee investment may be related to the external sources of information and advice available to employees. Interviews showed clearly that external financial advice was not consistent. A chargehand at a depot in East Anglia said he thought the buyout was a good thing at the time, but above all 'the banks were prepared to lend me the money and they wouldn't chuck money away'. However, a fitter in High Wycombe said, 'I was advised by an accountant friend that I would not get a good return.' Clearly, most financial institutions fully informed about the NFC's prospects and the availability of £200 interest-free loans were prepared to advise employee investment. Other sources may not have had access to the same information.

Two proxies for information were used in the questionnaire survey. The first was education, a potentially influential source of external informational asymmetry. Perhaps employees with longer educational histories

Table 5.9. *Relationship between age leaving full-time education and employee ownership*

	15 or under %	16–17 %	18 + %	Total %
Employee ownership				
Shareholders	38.7	40.9	100.0	45.4
Non-shareholders	61.3	50.1	0.0	54.6
% of sample	61.1	26.6	12.3	100.0
	(n = 93)	(n = 44)	(n = 15)	(n = 152)

Chi-square = 20.077, significant at 0.001 with 2 degrees of freedom.

Table 5.10. *Relationship between employee home ownership and share ownership*

	Owners %	Non-owners %	Total %
Employee ownership			
Shareholders	51.0	30.6	44.3
Non-shareholders	49.0	69.4	55.7
% of sample	67.1	32.9	100.0
	(n = 100)	(n = 49)	(n = 149)

Chi-square = 5.540, significant at 0.05 with 1 degree of freedom.

and/or some financial training had a better understanding of share participation and the events at the NFC at the time of the buyout. In fact, all employees in the sample who were in full-time education until at least the age of 18 were shareholders (Table 5.9). This category consisted entirely of managers, however, and represented only 12 per cent of the sample. Thus, the relationship, while statistically significant, has little explanatory power.

Of more relevance was the second indicator used: home ownership. It seems plausible that homeowners may have a more positive orientation towards share ownership and a better knowledge of what it involves. They may also have greater access to information from financial institutions than do private-rented or council tenants. As discussed earlier under the dependence hypothesis, a statistically significant relationship was not found between share ownership and housing status for the group of employees who had joined NFC before the buyout. But when the entire sample is divided into homeowners, a statistically significant relationship does emerge (Table 5.10).

Multivariate analysis

Next we investigated the relationships between significant variables in multivariate analysis, to determine how well these variables collectively explained the pattern of employee share ownership. In addition, an attempt was made to rank the explanatory variables in order of influence.

Two characteristics of the data, namely a dichotomous dependent variable (share ownership) and 'non-normal' variance due to mainly categorical independent variables, prevented the use of standard multivariate tests such as multiple regression. However, a special class of statistical tests has been formulated for the analysis of categorical data such as these. Loglinear models are useful for uncovering relationships among variables in multi-way cross-tabulations so they are similar to multiple regression.

The first step was to identify the significant explanatory variables from the bivariate analysis. Two emerged from the dependence hypothesis: previous work experience and children. Previous work experience was found to be highly correlated with occupation. Over 80 per cent of those with no previous work experience were white-collar employees and over 60 per cent had joined the NFC straight from school. The relationship between share ownership and the responsibility for young children was in the opposite direction to the one predicted. Of the significant variables from the bivariate analysis of the informational asymmetry hypothesis, education was found to be highly correlated with occupation. No manual employees were included in the 18-plus category for education. Consequently, these three variables (previous work experience, children and education) were omitted from the multivariate analysis.

The next stage was to investigate how well the four remaining significant explanatory variables generated by the informational asymmetry hypothesis, namely occupation (JOB), trade union membership (TUM), depot (BR) and housing tenure (HO), collectively explained the variation in share ownership, represented in this analysis by the scaled deviance. The effectiveness of any particular model fitted was represented by the amount it reduced the scaled deviance from the Grand Mean. As Table 5.11 shows, over 50 per cent of the scaled deviance was explained by the four-variable main effects model. This result was statistically significant to less than 0.001.

The next step was to investigate each variable individually. All four variables were highly significant, as predicted, but it seems that the effects of occupation (JOB) and trade union membership (TUM) were the strongest. The final stage of the analysis was an investigation of the effects of interaction terms, or second-order effects. Each second-order effect was

Table 5.11. *Logit analysis of the informational asymmetry hypothesis*

	Scaled deviance	Degrees of freedom	Probability
Model			
Grand mean	67.75	24	
JOB + TUM + BR + HO	32.12	18	p < 0.001
JOB	44.30	22	p < 0.001
TUM	53.93	23	p < 0.001
BR	58.09	22	p < 0.001
HO	62.04	23	p < 0.025
JOB + TUM + BR + HO			
+ JOB HO	28.86	16	not sig.
+ JOB TUM	28.86	16	not sig.
+ BR	28.60	14	not sig.
+ TUM	27.98	16	not sig.
+ TUM HO	29.93	17	not sig.
+ BR HO	27.59	16	not sig

where: JOB represents Occupation, TUM represents Trade Union Membership, BR represents Depot, HO represents Housing Tenure.

added to the main-effects model individually. As Table 5.11 shows, none of these terms appeared to have a statistically significant effect.

Summary of findings and conclusions

This chapter has investigated the employee investment decision. Two hypotheses were developed to explain why employees might choose to invest in their own company, and were tested against events at the NFC. The findings, particularly those from the questionnaire survey, support the information asymmetry hypothesis. Because information about the employee buyout was gradually disseminated from the Organising Committee to the manual workforce, there was plenty of time for suspicions to be aroused and the TGWU's influence to be maximised. The survey results also show that the four major predictor variables of the informational asymmetry hypothesis (occupation, trade union membership, depot and housing tenure) together explained over 50 per cent of the variation in share ownership among respondents. Dependence predictors, however, generally produced non-significant results. Employees with responsibility for children had a significantly lower propensity to invest than those without, but this was the opposite to what had been predicted in the proposition (although not beyond the broad dependence hypothesis' explanatory framework). Previous work experience also proved to be statistically significant in bivariate analysis. But the dependence hypothesis has weak explanatory power compared with the informational asymmetry hypothesis.

Rather than regard the two hypotheses as competing explanations for a certain set of events, one should use them to explain different sets of circumstances. It seems plausible that the circumstances of the NFC buyout, and events at BRS (Southern) where the questionnaire survey was administered, fit better into an informational framework. The threats to employment levels, or employee dependence on their current jobs, seemed to be lower at BRS (Southern) than elsewhere in the NFC or in other similar studies. Redundancies or closure had not been announced, the unit had been growing since 1981 and the problem of unemployment in the region was not as serious as elsewhere in Britain. Therefore, the dependence hypothesis may have failed in this study simply because it was inappropriate.

6

Employee ownership and industrial relations: issues

Introduction

At the theoretical level the employee ownership debate has revolved around two questions. The first is whether employee ownership significantly influences workplace industrial relations. It is sometimes argued that employee financial participation blurs the distinction between capital and labour, thereby changing the nature of the employment relationship enough to improve labour's input (Oakeshott, 1978; Cable and Fitzroy, 1980a, 1980b; Copeman et al., 1984). The result may be improved employee attitudes, more harmonious industrial relations and better economic performance in the firm. On the other hand, if unions strenuously resist employee ownership, industrial relations may be hurt by such a move.

The second major question of theoretical interest is whether employee ownership reduces variability of employment. That might occur if employee-owners became more flexible in their wage demands, so that the firm could respond to downturns by cutting wages rather than laying off employees.

Forms of ownership

In examining these questions empirically, it is important to recognise that different kinds of employee ownership are possible. One can distinguish individual versus collective, corporate versus cooperative, and majority versus partial forms of ownership.

Ownership is a multi-dimensional concept composed of a bundle of rights and functions (Dahl, 1970). The rights of profit, and of disposal and control are generally assumed to be conferred with ownership. In terms of a business organisation, the right to control includes (i) day-to-day internal control of the organisation, and (ii) a nominal right to participate in governing the firm.

In its fullest sense, ownership includes all these rights and functions, but they are rarely all conferred upon one group or individual in modern firms. The typical joint-stock company divides ownership rights and functions between shareholders who receive profit, disposal and nominal control rights, and the Board of Directors and executives who have internal control of the organisation.

This division of rights and functions has fragmented the concept of ownership to the extent that the distinction between ownership and control has been formalised. Consequently, the transfer of shareholder rights in most cases has no implications for control and vice versa. Similarly, there may be little connection between employee shareholding and employee control or voice, depending upon the model of employee ownership adopted. Here we define employee ownership as the involvement of employees in shareholder ownership rights and functions. Any changes in employee control or voice are viewed as events associated with industrial relations in a changed ownership environment, and are not included in the rights of employee ownership.

Until the last decade little attempt was made to classify the forms of employee involvement in shareholder ownership rights, or employee ownership. Now several typologies have been offered (Woodworth, 1981; Rothschild-Whitt, 1983; Toscano, 1983; Long, 1984; Bradley and Gelb, 1985). Three useful distinctions emerge from the literature. The first is between individual and social ownership. Individual ownership includes all models in which employees are permitted to hold an individual equity stake in the firm, which may be controlled directly by the individual. (This is the case at the NFC.) Social ownership includes all models of employee ownership in which a trust controls employees' shares collectively. Employees or their representatives participate in the administration and control of the trust.

In some cases of social ownership, the employees' shares are held in trust only temporarily at the beginning of a conversion. They are then transferred to individual accounts, either gradually or after a fixed retention period. In either cases, ownership is permanently conferred upon the beneficial trust so that the shareholder rights are limited to a share in the profits and increased participation in the trust's activities.

A second distinction is between cooperative and corporate models. In cooperative models, ownership is restricted to members, and employment is a prerequisite for membership. Each member is permitted one share which carries one vote and is entitled to a share of the profits. Membership expires when the employment contract ends. In corporate models, ownership is based on equity, and the nominal control rights and functions are allocated on the basis of one share–one vote, as in a conventional joint-stock company. A wide range of arrangements is possible under the corporate model of employee ownership. For example, profits may be allocated according to either the size of the equity stake or some other criterion. Neither model has fixed parameters for internal control. However, cooperative models of ownership tend to be associated with a greater allocation of control to employees.

A third distinction is between majority and partial employee ownership. It is helpful to think of employee ownership as a function of three components (Long, 1980): (i) the proportion of the company owned by employees; (ii) the proportion of the company that participates in ownership; and (iii) the concentration of ownership among employees.

The purest employee-owned firm is one which is 100 per cent owned by employees, with 100 per cent of the workforce participating in ownership and with an even distribution of ownership among the workforce. It is difficult to distinguish clearly between partial and majority employee ownership. Is a firm in which 80 per cent of employees own 40 per cent of the equity more or less employee-owned than one in which 40 per cent of employees own 80 per cent of the equity? Because of the multi-dimensional nature of the concept there is no *a priori* way of answering that question. Therefore, any definition of either partial or majority employee ownership should be treated with caution. For the purpose of this study, a majority employee-owned firm is one in which a majority of the equity is restricted to employees and in which 40 per cent of the employees have invested.

Theoretical studies

The empirical literature on the effects of employee ownership examined below focuses on individual forms of employee ownership, particularly those with corporate models. Theoretical frameworks for explaining the potential consequences of employee ownership have taken two main forms. Firstly, psychological models hypothesise associations between employee financial participation and employee attitudes and subsequent expected individual behavioural outcomes (Long, 1978a; Rhodes and Steers, 1981; Conte, 1982). Secondly, economic models hypothesise relationships between organisational forms and certain economic performance outcomes. These have included both micro- and macro-economic models (for example, Cable and Fitzroy, 1980a; 1980b; Weitzman, 1984; Meade, 1986; Estrin and Wilson, 1986).

94

Employee ownership issues

Psychological studies

Psychological studies have focused on attitudinal concepts such as organisational commitment, employee motivation and job satisfaction; and behavioural variables such as labour turnover, tardiness, absenteeism, etc. Long (1978a) hypothesised that individual employee share ownership increases employee organisational identification. This construct of organisational identification was composed of three inter-related concepts: integration defined as the degree to which an individual perceives that the attainment of organisational goals will result in personal satisfaction; involvement, defined as a sense of solidarity with or belonging to the organisation; and commitment defined as a sense of loyalty to the organisation.[1] The model predicted that employee share ownership improved commitment which directly improved behaviour supporting the organisation (e.g. lower labour turnover and grievances). Involvement and integration were also improved, leading to improved organisational performance, but the process also required improved motivation.[2]

Long's (1978a) model was primarily relevant to systems of individual share ownership in which the employee makes an actual financial investment. Alternatively, Rhodes and Steers (1981) designed their model specifically for producer cooperatives. They hypothesised that membership in a cooperative influenced employee perceptions of pay equity and participation in decision-making. The outcome was improved organisational commitment which subsequently improved individual behaviour leading to reductions in absenteeism and tardiness, etc.[3]

Conte's (1982) model borrowed from the other two, but was considerably more sophisticated. Like Rhodes and Steers' (1981), it was designed to be primarily applicable to cooperative or labour-managed firms. The model traced a similar path from the introduction of employee ownership through the individual's perceptions of employee ownership, to the effects on attitudinal motivators including commitment, identification and the meaningfulness of work. Employee ownership was seen as improving individual performance including effort levels which led to improved organisational performance. But the model improved on the others in one important respect: it was far more sensitive to moderating variables. For example, the reasons for worker ownership were hypothesised to moderate the relationships between worker ownership and the perception of worker ownership, and between worker ownership and any structure of worker participation. A similar point was made by Bradley and Gelb (1983a) in their survey of the empirical evidence on the effects of different models of employee ownership on productivity. In many of the American employee buyouts where cost reduction was not exigent, the extent of performance improvements due to the changed ownership structure was not so clear.

Economic studies

The economic models have adapted micro- and macro-economic theory to develop hypotheses about the outcomes of employee share ownership and profit-sharing for organisational performance and the economy. Three main approaches have been adopted which largely overlap in both their expected outcomes and their mechanisms. Firstly, employee financial participation could help create a share economy in which an excess demand for labour is created that may cure stagflation. Secondly, employee financial participation may encourage greater wage flexibility which may increase employment at both the micro- and macro-economic level. Thirdly, employee financial participation may restructure incentives sufficiently to improve labour productivity.

The first two of these approaches have been dominated by macro-economic theory with only indirect implications for industrial relations. Since the late 1950s, a body of literature on the macro-economic effects of a cooperative economy has developed (for example, Ward, 1958; Vanek, 1970; Clayre, 1980; Jay, 1980). However, the debate in the mid-1980s about the macro-economic effects of employee financial participation has been dominated by Weitzman's (1984) innovative solution to the problem of stagflation in Western industrial economies. He viewed labour market rigidity as the main cause of stagflation, and especially the wage system in which employee remuneration remained fixed regardless of firm performance.[4] 'The lasting solution to stagflation requires going inside the workings of a modern capitalist economy and correcting the underlying structural flaw directly at the level of the firm by changing the nature of labor remuneration' (Weitzman, 1984: p. 3). Weitzman advocated an alternative macro-economy that would induce an excess demand for labour. At least 20 per cent of workers' pay would be linked to an index of firm performance, either revenue or profits, so that an employee's overall remuneration fluctuated according to firm performance. The dynamic mechanism of a share economy created the correct incentives to achieve the desired outcome, i.e. to conquer stagflation, and create a permanent excess demand for labour.[5]

Meade (1986) developed Weitzman's model a stage further whilst taking a different starting-point. He viewed the 'them and us' division between capital and labour as a major source of inefficiency. The share economy eroded the division somewhat, but also generated other conflicts of interest. Meade accepted that the economy would function as Weitzman predicted during recession. But as the economy improved and profits rose conflicts would arise between 'insiders' and 'outsiders'. Employers would be willing to take on more workers, but employees would have an incentive to keep new entrants out, as taking on new employees would dilute the portion of revenue to go to labour. A similar conflict would result over investment decisions.[6]

Meade (1986) advocated his own share economy which aimed to minimise the conflicts of interest based on Labour-Capital Partnerships (LCP) with share certificates for both capital and labour in proportion to their respective current incomes. Both would carry entitlement to the same rate of dividend. However, LCPs would abandon the non-discriminatory principle of pay.

Changing the wages system has profound implications for industrial relations. But Weitzman (1984) made little attempt to explain the effects of his model on industrial relations. He did concede that employee share-holding may boost morale and foster a sense of partnership at the firm level which could improve productivity, but was sceptical of the macro-economic effects of improved industrial relations (Weitzman, 1984: p. 143).

Trade unions may well have a more fundamental impact upon the share economy. The low basic wage upon which the share economy depends may provoke trade union resistance to its implication. Then if excess demand for labour is created, trade unions may push wages up as increased wages would not affect employment (Jackman, 1985).

The wage flexibility argument bears some similarities to the Weitzman-type model, but is a considerable dilution of it. It is the argument adopted in the British government Green Paper (1986), *Profit Related Pay*, and included in the Finance Act 1987. The government's position appears to be primarily a response to the need to stimulate employment and facilitate adjustment on the down-cycle. Increasing flexibility may reduce fluctuations in employment levels. Under a fixed wage system a contraction in demand for a firm's product impels the employer to contract the workforce. Under a flexible wage system a reduction in the firm's overall wage bill could be achieved by reducing the profit or revenue-related element of employees' remuneration which would minimise redundancies. In such an economy the pressures of stagflation would be reduced and periods of lost production avoided.

A major criticism of the wage flexibility approach has been that a critical mass is required for success. Otherwise where an excess demand for labour exists, competition between firms will force wage levels up and perhaps even lead to the familiar wage system.

The third economic approach, focusing on incentives and productivity, has a more direct bearing on industrial relations. A conventional assumption in micro-economic theory is that inputs have fixed specifications and yield a fixed performance. The maximisation of allocative efficiency (for example, obtaining the best price for a factor of production) is therefore viewed as the key to maximising productivity and output. However, in the case of labour, this assumption need not hold. The utilisation of labour as a factor of production, its X-efficiency, may be sub-optimal whilst allocative efficiency remains high. Leibenstein (1966) suggests that over-emphasis on allocative efficiency may have obscured the possibility of dramatic improvements in productivity, achieved by using different incentive systems to improve labour's X-efficiency. This proposition also questioned the behavioural model of economic activity which identified individual financial incentives as the way to maximise effort levels.[7]

The consideration of non-financial employee incentives and improved productivity in economics emerged from studies of labour-managed firms (Vanek, 1970; Meade, 1972). In conventional firms with a fixed wage system, employees had little incentive to perform above the level required to retain the job. Under a labour-managed firm there were two incentives: the financial incentives of profit-sharing which linked performance and rewards; and social or participatory motivation which bolstered the financial incentives. Individual and associative incentives were viewed as complementary. In small firms both were influential. In larger firms, however, the link between individual rewards and firm performance was too weak to trigger increased efforts and might even have the dysfunctional effect of encouraging free-riding (Alchian and Demsetz, 1972; Jensen and Meckling, 1979). Strong associative incentives might be needed to compensate for the diluted effects of the financial incentives.

Cable and Fitzroy (1980a; 1980b) took the impact of social interaction factors on economic incentives a stage further to include worker collusion in trade unions. The conflict between capital and labour engendered low-trust relationships which resulted in negative collusion by workers in trade unions to restrict output or reduce productive efficiency. But there might be a way of transforming negative collusion into positive collusion to maximise joint wealth: by employee participation in decision-making and profit-sharing, both of which are group incentives.

Although Cable and Fitzroy (1980a; 1980b) were sensitive to issues such as shirking and horizontal supervision, and the importance of employee perceptions of their ability to influence managerial decisions, they stopped short of a hypothesis about industrial relations effects of worker participation. Instead they considered the relationship between worker participation or profit-sharing schemes and measurements of productive efficiency. However, their work provides a starting-point for a theory about the effects of employee ownership on industrial relations.

Theoretical problems

The psychological and economic approaches are best viewed as complementary rather than as alternatives. Nevertheless, even when the two approaches are combined, several problems remain.

Firstly, there are no standard definitions of the relevant variables. In the psychological literature, for example, terms like commitment and identification overlap but can mean different things, and might be interpreted differently by different readers. This makes comparisons of empirical findings problematic.

Secondly, concepts such as commitment tend to be multi-dimensional which produces measurement and weighting problems. Furthermore, existing theory says little about the underlying causes of these attitudes. For example, does an employee identify with a firm out of fear of job loss, pride, or monetary rewards? In this study we attempt to reduce these biases by dividing attitudinal variables into unidimensional measures.

Thirdly, economic models are constrained by their specifications. An association between ownership and changes in economic performances does not mean that employee ownership causes the changes. Events outside the models' specification may have generated economic performance changes independently. Moreover, most performance studies do not attempt to explain the mechanisms by which individual share ownership in an employee-owned firm affects participants. Individual attitudinal and behavioural changes are simply derived from performance indicators.

The psychological studies examine these processes more closely, but they also encounter a problem of causality. Multivariate analysis techniques can control the effects of intervening variables in cross-sectional data, but causality is more effectively tested through longitudinal data. However, longitudinal data is rare and difficult to obtain. Ideally one would like to be able to predict where a conversion to employee ownership is likely to occur long enough in advance to negotiate access during a period of change and uncertainty, and to administer a successful attitude survey both before and after the change in ownership. Economic data may be easier to collect longitudinally so the two approaches might best be considered as complementary.

Even this compatibility of the two approaches cannot compensate for a hiatus in the theoretical literature: a model for explaining the effects of employee ownership on the institutions and processes of industrial relations. Efforts have been made to explain the effects of employee ownership on trade unionism (Stern, 1982; Bradley and Gelb, 1983a). However, only one attempt has been made to develop a theoretical framework for labour–management relations in employee-owned organisations. Bradley and Gelb (1983b; 1987) compared the organisational characteris-

99

tics of the Mondragon group of cooperatives in Spain and a large Japanese firm. Mondragon's personnel policies resembled those of the Japanese corporation in a number of ways including a commitment to life-time employment; an emphasis on socialisation into firm ideology; high labour flexibility within the enterprise; comprehensive social benefits during employment; and a substantial annual bonus allocated to employees from profits.

Bradley and Gelb (1987) compared the adjustment processes of cooperative and mixed economies during recession with emphasis upon the role of labour institutions. They suggested that the labour market in a cooperative economy adjusted more quickly to a fall in profits, etc.

The question of participation may also be relevant to a hypothesis about the industrial relations effects of employee share ownership. Employee ownership is often associated with increased participation, and the failure of some forms of employee ownership is often attributed to a failure to include increased worker participation. Participation in management may release the power of democratic institutions. Channels are created for information-processing and conflict resolution which may reduce organisational inefficiencies (Levin, 1982; Jones and Svejnar, 1985).

The debate about the relative merits of employee share ownership and participation and their interaction is beyond the scope of this study. But it may be worth noting one point which is largely overlooked in the literature: the actual level of employee participation following the conversion may be less than anticipated. This issue is discussed in Chapter 7.

At the NFC, the change in ownership was not accompanied by any major change in employee involvement in decision-making, other than as shareholders. Consequently any changes in attitude can be viewed as a direct result of ownership. In addition, the buyout leaders stressed that there would be little change in organisational or decision-making structures following a buyout, so false expectations were not raised. Thus our hypotheses on the effects of a conversion to employee ownership on industrial relations are primarily applicable to firms with corporate decision-making structures.

Empirical studies

Empirical studies have taken two main forms which correspond with the theoretical models discussed above.[8] Firstly, the effects of employee ownership have been measured by company performance indicators such as productivity, profits, employment and investment. Secondly, those effects have been measured by changes, if any, in employee attitudes and individual behaviour and by comparisons of the attitudes of employee-shareholders and control groups. Both comparative and case study approaches have been employed in the two types of research. Case studies in particular have often used non-shareholders in the organisation as a control group for attitudinal tests.

Evidence has been collected from a number of organisations in North America, Europe and Australia. Overall, the empirical evidence suggests the potential for employee ownership to achieve its objectives, for example, to improve employee attitudes, harmonise industrial relations and raise firm performance. However, the evidence is often ambiguous. One source of confusion has been the need to distinguish between different models of employee ownership. To highlight the features of the National Freight Company model of employee ownership, this review confines itself to describing the empirical evidence in companies resembling the NFC, particularly in combining share ownership with a corporate structure.

Performance studies

On balance, the few studies which investigate the economic performance of organisations under corporate models of individual employee ownership give a positive endorsement to such schemes. In the United States, the National Center for Employee Ownership claims that 'there is no major study that shows a negative relationship between employee ownership and productivity'. Tannenbaum and Conte (1976) compared the performances of three groups of US firms: conventional firms; firms with Employee Stock Ownership Plans (ESOPs) in 75 per cent of which workers owned at least 50 per cent of equity, but in trusts; and majority employee-owned firms with individual ownership. The employee-owned firms appeared to perform better than the conventional firms. The 30 individual employee-owned firms appeared to perform better than the ESOPs, and had an average level of profitability 1.7 times higher than the control group. This finding should be treated with caution as the results were not statistically significant and there may have been self-selection in the sample.

The effects of employee ownership on performance are more ambiguous for the corporate models with partial employee ownership. One study of ESOPs in the United States suggested that firms with employee share ownership schemes were less profitable than firms without such schemes (Livingston and Henry, 1980). This study is, however, exceptional. Brooks, Henry and Livingston (1982) compared 51 large ESOPs with a matched sample of conventional firms and found no statistically significant differences in profitability. Marsh and McAllister's (1981) survey of 229 ESOPs, 80 per cent of which are not majority employee-owned, found that those firms' aggregate productivity increase was above the national

101

average, but was attributable solely to the performance of the medium-sized firms in the sample. Neither voting rights, the proportion of employee-owners, nor the proportion of shares held by the trust were related to productivity. Only 59 per cent perceived any improvement in employee morale; 36 per cent reported a fall in labour turnover, and 32 per cent an improvement in quality of work. The survey, however, may have had a self-selection bias as many firms did not respond.

Bradley and Estrin (1988) provide the first substantial performance study of a majority employee-owned British firm but with a collective ownership model. This study of the John Lewis Partnership (JLP) investigates the influence of the company's unique ownership and organisational arrangements on its commercial performance, both in absolute terms and relative to its major competitors. Their principal finding is that, far from being a hindrance, such arrangements have given the JLP significant advantages in the market-place. The Partnership performs well relative to the sector and the economy as a whole, and is comparable with the other leading enterprises in retailing and distribution.

Little empirical evidence exists about the effects of the main form of partial employee ownership, the approved share-based profit-sharing schemes. Firm conclusions are difficult to reach. Richardson and Nejad (1986) measured the share price movements of 41 firms in the multiple stores sector during 1978–84. The 23 firms that had introduced some form of employee financial participation scheme outperformed those without schemes, and the difference was significant at the 10 per cent level. When the share price movements of enthusiastic participators and traditional firms were compared, the former increased on average by 26 per cent during 1978–84 and the latter on average by only 15 per cent, a difference significant at the 5 per cent level. However, as causality could not be determined, 'it may well be that the innovating firms introduced, or extended, financial participation as part of a much wider review of their management strategy. In this case, the use of financial participation might be an excellent index of improved management but not the sole cause of, or even an important contributor to, improved performance' (Richardson and Nejad, 1986: p. 247). This point is emphasised by Wadhwani and Wall (1988) who conducted a more rigorous study on similar issues.

Other studies have taken employment and wage determination as their indicators of the effectiveness of employee financial participation. Estrin and Wilson (1986) investigated 52 small to medium-sized engineering and metal-working firms in the Midlands and North England, comparing firms which had introduced profit-sharing schemes during 1978–82 and those which had not. Profit-sharing firms differed little from the control group in their decisions about pay or employment, but did appear to have better corporate performance, with higher factor productivity and rates of return on capital. In addition, profit-sharing firms appeared to have higher unionisation and more harmonious labour relations with lower quit rates and working days lost. But the difficulty of inferring causality led the authors to conclude that better managed firms with better labour morale were more likely to introduce profit-sharing. Simultaneous estimations of labour demand and wage equations suggested that when controlling for firm-specific variables, employment was 13 per cent higher in the profit-sharing group. Similarly, profit-sharing firms appeared to depress wages by some 4 per cent. Although findings were preliminary, Estrin and Wilson (1986) give some support to Weitzman's predictions about employment (discussed above), but shed no light on the dynamic process of firm adjustment through the trade cycle.

Blanchflower and Oswald (1986a; 1986b) also tested the effects of employee share schemes on employment levels and capital investment, but reached opposite conclusions to Estrin and Wilson (1986). Their samples were the private manufacturing sectors in the Workplace Industrial Relations Survey 1980 and 1984. Measurements of employment and investment were based on managerial perceptions rather than objective company data. Furthermore, the 1980 survey did not differentiate the types of schemes, but treated all as one variable. Both the 1980 and the 1984 survey results suggested that employee share schemes made no difference to firms' employment and investment.

Case studies of employee buyouts have also included performance data (for example, Long, 1978a; Hammer and Stern, 1980; Bradley and Gelb, 1983a). But the effects of conversion cannot be tested simply by examining performance. The advantage of case studies is that they can reveal the circumstances in which conversion took place and provide detailed insights into whether the new ownership structure has contributed to any changes in performance. Bradley and Gelb (1983a) summarised a number of transitions to employee ownership using such a case history approach. They found that in many of the North American buyouts, cost reduction and productivity improvements were not exigent, as many of the conversions were corporate divestitures of moderately profitable firms. Firms in this category made only moderate workforce performance improvements. In the weaker firms, which included the British cases of the Scottish News Enterprises, Meriden Motorcycle Cooperative and Kirby Manufacturing and Engineering Company Ltd, structural changes and improved work intensity were required for viability. In these three cases, unit labour costs were reduced by 20 to 30 per cent. Although the initial impact of a conversion may be to raise labour productivity, Bradley and Gelb argue that the effect is probably not due to employee ownership *per se* but depends on 'the extent of reorganisation effected in the transition' (Bradley and Gelb, 1983a: p. 51).

Attitude studies

The main attitudinal variables measured in empirical studies have been employee motivation, organisational commitment and job satisfaction. There have been few studies of the effects of employee share ownership on these variables in individual employee-owned firms with corporate models. In the studies that do exist, findings suggest that employee-shareholders display significantly higher levels of commitment, involvement and integration than non-shareholders (Long, 1978a; 1978b; Goldstein, 1978; Russell et al., 1979). But statistically significant differences do not always emerge between shareholders and non-shareholders in their motivation (Long, 1978a; 1980; 1981). Members of the so-called scavenger cooperatives in San Francisco have higher levels of motivation than non-members, although motivation levels do not differ significantly between scavenger members and employees form the public companies (Russell et al., 1979).[9] In the only longitudinal study of employee attitudes in a firm converted to employee ownership – a Canadian electronics firm in which 33 per cent of shares went to 83 per cent of eligible employees – Long (1981) found that employee motivation did not change between the administration of the first two questionnaires, but dropped significantly between the second and the third administrations. Similarly at Byers Transport Limited and Saratoga Knitting, statistically significant differences do not emerge between the motivation levels of shareholders and non-shareholders.[10] Also, Kruse's (1984) study of ESOPs finds little effect upon employee motivation. The schemes introduced in his two case studies do not give employees voting rights which seems to have a considerable impact on the effectiveness of the plans.

In Britain, few attitude surveys of the effects of the approved employee share schemes have been undertaken (Wallace Bell and Hanson, 1984; 1987; Copeman Paterson, 1986). In their 1984 study Wallace Bell and Hanson questioned some 2,700 employees in twelve firms with profit-sharing schemes. Eighty-six per cent of respondents agree that such a scheme is good for the company and its employees. Ninety-three per cent say the scheme is popular because people like to have the bonus and 76 per cent agree that it makes people take a greater interest in profits and financial results. Some 51 per cent suggest the scheme encourages people to work more effectively whilst 96 per cent believe it should not be seen as a substitute for wages.[11] The authors conclude that

Profit-sharing is not a panacea, but an increasing number of companies believe that a well-designed profit sharing scheme can in fact help to secure genuine employee commitment. We think that the results of our survey, the most thorough and extensive of its kind ever to be conducted in the United Kingdom, support that view. (Wallace Bell and Hanson, 1984: p. 11)

However, a close examination of the findings suggests a more cautious conclusion. The scoring procedure employed a scale of responses to represent the strength of an individual's attitude. The numbers of those who agree strongly with the statements, the only clearly positive indication of support for the scheme, are low. Only 11 per cent agree strongly that profit-sharing makes people take a greater interest in profits and financial results, 14 per cent that it is good for the company and employees, and 6 per cent that it encourages people to work more effectively.

A second survey, undertaken by the management consultants Copeman Paterson (1986) on behalf of the Wider Share Ownership Council, examines managers' attitudes towards employee share schemes in 138 companies. The results are again presented descriptively. The study separates responses relating to the profit-sharing schemes and savings-related (SAYE) schemes. The overall effect of the profit-sharing schemes seems to have a greater influence on attitudes. Seventy-seven per cent of respondents perceive at least some effect of the profit-sharing scheme upon 'improved loyalty or attitudes', compared with 60 per cent for the SAYE scheme. For productivity increases, the figures are 45 per cent and 27 per cent respectively. Forty-four per cent and 35 per cent respond that the schemes facilitate recruitment, and 40 per cent and 20 per cent suggest that they facilitate negotiations. However, only 11 per cent and 10 per cent feel the schemes increase interest in and understanding of company performance. A repeat survey in 1987 produced similar findings.

A survey by the Department of Employment into the extent, objectives and effects of profit-sharing and share ownership schemes in Britain also disaggregates the types of schemes, although findings are again based on managerial perceptions (Smith, 1986). Telephone interviews were conducted with 1,125 companies with a turnover of £0.75 million or over. Later 303 of these firms were interviewed in greater depth; of these 191 had an all-employee scheme. Results suggest that the schemes generally satisfy the company's objectives which include making employees more committed to the company, profit conscious and cooperative.

The results from these surveys are disappointing to advocates of employee financial participation in Britain. Some have argued that the full impact of employee share schemes is not being registered. Researchers at Glasgow University argue: 'Our doubts concerning attitude surveys have led us to a conviction that only case studies, providing qualitatively richer information from a variety of indicative and interview sources and considering the performance and development of schemes over time, can hope to give a more practically useful insight' (cited in Incomes Data Services, 1986: p. 8). Perhaps the two most important cases of employee ownership in capitalist democracies are the Mondragon Group of Cooperatives in the Basque region of Spain and the John Lewis Partnership in Britain. This experience has been encouraging.

The Mondragon cooperatives

Since its origins in the mid-1950s, the Mondragon Group has grown to include 160 cooperatives, with gross sales of £380 million and 19,000 individual members. Productive activity is concentrated in manufacturing, with an emphasis on consumer durables. Products range from appliances and bicycles to machine tools, electrical components and bus bodies. The Group includes its own banking system, research and development complex, technical training schools and a social security organisation.

When a person wishes to join a Mondragon cooperative, he or she must make an initial capital investment; for the lower-paid members, the stake is roughly equivalent to a year's pay. Each year the Group's profits (after set-asides to fund the Collective Reserves and Social Fund) are distributed among the workers' capital accounts. At retirement, the worker-owner must draw out his or her accumulated profit within two years. (Retired workers also receive pensions from the Group.) Members may not sell their shares, and if they leave the Group before retirement age, they may sacrifice part of their accumulated profits.

Mondragon's business success testifies to the viability of this form of ownership. Since the mid-1970s its profit rate has been considerably higher than the average industrial profit rate for the Basque region. Thomas and Logan (1982) found that the Group had done better than other local firms in all years but 1971. Some of its enterprises have achieved significant market share positions (up to 30 per cent in some consumer durables), and the limited sales volume of others reflects a deliberate decision to keep the size of the organisational unit relatively small.

Mondragon's experience appears to bear out the notion that employee ownership can promote efficiency. In comparison with conventional firms, there is little social differentiation between managers and workers in the cooperative. Because of Mondragon's compressed pay scale, managers could earn much more in other firms; recognising the financial sacrifices that managers make in order to remain in the Group, workers are more inclined to trust them.

106

In many respects, the enterprises are quite conventionally run, and the firms are generally viewed as well-disciplined work environments. The discipline is due not only to workers' respect for management, but to an institutional emphasis on self-management. In some enterprises, workers take a 90-hour course that instructs them in the structure and economics of the enterprise. Information on current performance is freely shared with all members of the firm. Peer pressure is a significant factor in keeping all members working efficiently.

Mondragon has not been immune to pressures in the larger economy. Its rate of profit declined almost steadily from 1973 to 1981, and it continued to make losses through 1984. Other industrial enterprises in the Basque region performed even worse during this period, however, and were less able to keep their workers employed. Spanish industrial employment declined steadily from 1976 to 1983, while the number of members in the Mondragon Group increased about 20 per cent over that period.

That increase in Mondragon's employment was made possible by holding down wages. In 1979 pay levels on established Mondragon cooperatives were about 10 per cent higher than the national norm. Thereafter, while the overall Spanish wage level remained roughly constant through 1983, pay on these Mondragon cooperatives dropped sharply, to a level 5 per cent below the national norm in 1980, and remained below the Spanish average through 1983. Between 1980 and 1983, pay cuts in some cooperatives (including unpaid overtime and givebacks of two months' salary) recapitalised the equivalent of one-quarter of fixed assets, enabling the enterprises to avoid taking on debt.

The Mondragon experience suggests that a cooperative may be able to respond more rapidly and flexibly than conventional firms to changes in economic conditions. Since labour and capital are not at odds with one another, but are identical, the cooperative can operate as a single decision-maker. Giving its commitment to maintaining employment and promoting regional employment, Mondragon has exercised its flexible response capability by reducing workers' compensation quickly during a downturn, safeguarding the long-term viability of an enterprise that represents members' capital investment as well as their source of employment (Bradley and Gelb, 1987).

The John Lewis Partnership

Employees of the John Lewis Partnership (JLP) own the enterprise collectively through an employee trust. This large UK retail chain, established in the nineteenth century, was converted to its current ownership structure in 1929 by its founder, who believed that a profit-sharing arrangement would tend to increase labour productivity. (He also believed in the principle that there should be an upper bound on the return to capital.) By fiscal 1987 the Partnership had achieved a turnover of almost £1.6 billion and profits of about £400 million. With more than 30,000 employees (partners), it is comparable in size to the NFC.

Each year partners receive a portion of the company's profit, originally in the form of interest-bearing shares and since 1970 as cash bonuses. The bonus has historically represented a significant part of total compensation, typically exceeding 20 per cent of basic pay in recent years. Unlike members of the NFC and the Mondragon cooperatives, who have individual capital stakes in their enterprise, JLP partners have no right to redeem their shares in the trust when they leave the company.

The founder of the John Lewis Partnership regarded a strong management role as essential to keep profit-hungry workers from maximising short-term gains while neglecting investment for the future. The company is run by a chairman, who appoints a majority of the company's executive board. (In theory the chairman can be removed from the Central Council, 80 per cent of whose members are elected by the current partners.) To encourage a long-term perspective among the partners, the firm tries to keep them well informed about the company's situation and alternatives. A concern for equity (and harmony) is also evident in the written constitution that governs employee–management relations in the Partnership. All in all, the company's democratic structures do not seriously impede effective day-to-day management.

The John Lewis Partnership is good to its employees, paying about as much as its major competitors (GUS, Marks and Spencer, Sainsbury, and Tesco) even before the substantial bonus is taken into account, and maintaining somewhat greater stability in employment. Unlike the other firms, which shed labour during the 1974–6 recession, the JLP never actually reduced the size of its work force. JLP's nominal wages have been relatively stable, with the bonus varying more significantly with changing market-place conditions.

Some critics of employee ownership have argued that it will discourage appropriate reinvestment, since worker-owners will take a short-term view and insist on immediate payout of all profits. The governance structure of the John Lewis Partnership appears to have avoided this difficulty. In terms of both sales and profits, the JLP has grown at about the same rate as its principal competitors, funded in part by significant retained earnings. Since 1971, between 12 and 18 per cent of value added has been retained within the firm each year.

In comparison with its fastest growing competitors, the John Lewis Partnership increased its employment and fixed assets relatively slowly.

That is, JLP achieved superior growth in factor productivity. Its rate of return on capital over the period 1970-87 grew at a rate of 2.1 per cent, compared with 0.3 per cent for Sainsbury and declines for the other three competitors. When JLP's two basic lines of business – High Street stores and the Waitrose supermarket chain – are analysed separately, its superior performance is even more striking (Bradley and Estrin, 1988).

Hypothesis: effects of employee ownership on industrial relations

In this study two possible outcomes from a conversion to employee ownership are hypothesised. Firstly, that individual share ownership will harmonise labour relations. Secondly, that share ownership will generate new tensions in a workforce and consequently prove to be dysfunctional. The actual impact on industrial relations would be expected to vary with the precise nature of employee ownership. We focus here on the majority employee-owned firm with individual shareholdings and a corporate model.

Employee ownership harmonises labour relations

Employee ownership may improve labour relations in at least two ways. Firstly, it may change the structure of financial incentives, and the actual amount of a worker's financial rewards. Secondly, employee ownership may create or heighten a sense of identification with, or commitment to, the company, and hence a greater feeling of responsibility in the pursuit of joint wealth maximisation. Whether an employee takes shares to protect his job or to seek capital gains, the financial stake may reduce the perceived gap between individual rewards, both financial and non-financial, and the company's objectives. This change in perception may in turn engender more cooperative industrial relations. If employees also believe that individual efforts can influence company performance and therefore improve personal rewards, their attitudes and behaviour may be affected in at least three ways. Firstly, individual self-monitoring may improve, leading to increased cost consciousness, better-quality work and greater effort levels. Secondly, employees may increase their horizontal monitoring of others in their work group. This scrutiny will tend to reduce free-riding, particularly in small groups, as it imposes losses on fellow workers. More positively, employees will be more willing to assist others to learn new on-the-job productive skills, which may harmonise industrial relations and improve productivity. The overall effect will be to reduce supervision costs. Thirdly, management shareholders may increase vertical monitoring as reflected both in standards of supervision at the workplace, and in corporate management decisions.

However, several variables could distort these relationships, so that individual employee share ownership in a buyout may have little or no effect on a shareholder's attitudes and industrial relaitions. The size of an individuals's holding may not be large enough to reduce perceptions of the differences between an individual's rewards and a company's objectives. Further, any income from share ownership is likely to be small compared with salaries and wages, and is therefore also unlikely to affect financial incentives. Consequently, an individual employee-shareholder may retain allegiances to the traditional institutions of labour-management relations in a firm. The size of the firm, and particularly an individual's linkage with profit centres, may also obscure the relationship between individual efforts and rewards based on improved company performance, so that the link in individual perceptions is far less meaningful than, for example, in piece-rate systems.

In such situations employee ownership may not trigger the incentives to change attitudes. In addition it may be that a certain threshold proportion of a workforce must take shares in order to: (i) make workers feel they are part of an employee-owned firm; and (ii) legitimise any additional horizontal or vertical monitoring which may result.

In some cases, then, attitudes may be unaffected by employee ownership, or if an association exists between employee ownership and attitudes, it may not be reflected in individual or group behaviour.

Employee ownership destabilises labour relations

A less conventional but plausible hypothesis is that industrial relations may deteriorate as a consequence of employee ownership. There are at least two potential sources of tension: (i) a division in a workforce between employee-shareholders and non-shareholders; and (ii) a gap between employees' expectations of ownership and actual outcomes.

If employee share ownership is not widely dispersed, a division in a workforce between shareholders and non-shareholders may generate new tensions rather than harmonise labour relations. After a conversion, there may be pressure to restrain wage increases in order to allow high dividend payments to shareholders, particularly in view of specific tax advantages. If a significant proportion of the workforce does not invest, their resistance to this pressure could create tensions during collective bargaining. Also, if the conversion to employee ownership succeeds in creating large capital gains for shareholders, non-shareholders may become resentful; on the other hand, an unsuccessful conversion may intensify horizontal and vertical monitoring, possibly worsening labour relations. Further tension could arise if the shareholders' rights of ownership are extended in practice at the workplace, particularly to issues such as promotion, job security and redundancy priorities. If share ownership creates a two-tier workforce, tensions between employees may increase.

A second source of conflict may be related to shareholders' expectations from the rights of ownership. Employee-shareholders may expect ownership to include, at the minimum, rights to profit, rights of disposal, and voting rights (although the last has often been denied in Employee Stock Ownership Plans in the United States). Beyond the typical rights associated with ordinary shares in joint-stock companies, employee-shareholders may have high expectations of increased participation in decision-making, perhaps looking forward to new participatory institutions such as works councils or consultative committees, greater disclosure of information and a greater management responsiveness to workforce demands. If these expectations are disappointed, industrial relations may suffer.

Such expectations are likely, by definition, to be met in cooperative models of employee ownership. Conversely, the introduction of a partial employee ownership scheme under corporate models, particularly in profit-sharing and employee share schemes, is unlikely to arouse hopes of greatly increased worker participation in decision-making, and the company is unlikely to introduce such innovations independently. The potential for disappointment is greatest in the majority-owned firms with corporate models. However, if expectations of increased employee participation are not raised, then a conversion to employee ownership need not be accompanied by new mechanisms for participation and will not lead to new conflicts. Similarly, if the expectations raised can be met, then disharmony can be averted.

7

The effects of employee share ownership on industrial relations at the NFC

Introduction

This chapter presents the empirical findings relating to the effects of employee share ownership upon employee attitudes and industrial relations at the NFC. It examines both the interview and questionnaire data to test the two hypotheses developed in Chapter 6. The evidence supports the hypothesis that employee ownership harmonises industrial relations. The chapter concludes with an evaluation of the NFC's performance since the change in ownership, which reinforces the conclusion that employee ownership at the NFC has had positive effects.

Industrial relations at the NFC

Labour relations in the road freight transport industry present a mixed picture. Regulation may have improved some of the conditions of employment, but at the expense of labour flexibility and harmonious industrial relations in certain locations. Between 1948 and 1968, BRS was one of the most strike-prone of the nationalised industries. An average 220 days per 1,000 employees were lost each year between 1950 and 1968, and this figure was doubled by major strikes in 1951 and 1960.[1]

The road freight transport industry in the 1930s had been run by employers who had scant regard for working conditions, safety or the maintenance of vehicles. 'The employers were individualistic in their attitude; competition between them was fierce, and undercutting, the payment of low wages and the systematic evasion of regulations common practice' (Bullock, 1960: p.545). Moreover, employees were often willing to collaborate with employers to improve their own returns. Consequently, unionisation had been low.[2]

The Transport Act 1947 which nationalised road haulage activities established complete collective bargaining and consultation machinery.

This new system was successfully implemented and permanently retained; thus BRS and its successor, the National Freight Corporation, had a separate and independent machinery.

Labour relations and conditions of employment were formalised, with mixed results. BRS' conditions of employment and basic wage rates were slightly superior to those of most private hauliers. BRS employees also received bonuses. Employee influence was channelled through the trade unions which remained active in the organisation through joint consultation procedures. From the late 1950s, BRS was also a pioneer of productivity bargaining.[3]

On the other hand, nationalisation substituted bureaucratic procedures and strict adherence to regulations, particularly at the larger depots, for the informal arrangements which had prevailed earlier in many hauliers. This change was frustrating to drivers accustomed to collaborating with owner/managers to evade regulations.[4] Drivers in the private sector often earned more in a working week, as the statutory maximum working week was strictly enforced at BRS, whereas private hauliers may have been prepared to overlook regulations. Indeed, 'despite all the regulations imposed on road haulage many traces of pre-war practices survived well into the 1950s and well beyond' (Goodman, 1979: p. 92).

Thus regulation in the public sector may have disharmonised industrial relations, although the problems were mainly in the larger depots, as Chapter 5 suggested.

Qualitative findings

Company performance data from the NFC suggests that employee ownership and improved communications have improved employee motivation and industrial relations. The interview data presents more mixed results. Senior management enthusiastically believe that share ownership improved employee motivation by linking rewards with the company's success. However, at lower levels in the organisation, the motivational effects were more cautiously appraised. Interviewees felt that the incentives for increased effort were greater for senior management than for lower-level employees. One branch manager felt that 'senior management are now prepared to invest more and there is more risk-taking'. Similarly another manager felt that 'the buyout has made a difference to performance, but this has come from the top. Lower down there's been no difference.' Where positive changes had occurred at the shop-floor level, managers often drew a distinction between changed attitudes and improved employee performance. According to a branch manager, 'Attitudes have changed since the buyout, not performance. People aren't going to work any harder because of share ownership, but attitudes towards customers have changed.'

Other managers said that employee-shareholders showed new interest in the company's business, which had numerous beneficial effects; workers were more likely to gather market information about the potential for future contracts and the activities of competitors, and suggest ways to improve work methods. These suggestions were expressed both formally through the Local Joint Committee and informally in conversations.

Some managers felt that employee ownership had brought no positive changes at all but might have created some problems. 'Not a thing has changed', said one. 'There may be more emphasis on image and customer presentation, but that's nothing to do with the buyout.' In terms of industrial relations some interviewees expressed concern about a possible division in the workforce. One manager thought that 'the buyout has split employees into "haves" and "have-nots" in terms of those who are interested in seeing their investments grow and those that didn't invest'. The potential split in the workforce could also result in dual rights. The same manager reluctantly admitted: 'It's hard to sack a shareholder. Nobody is meant to know who owns shares, but the pay checks include a deduction for the interest-free loan so we know, and they know that we know.'

Managers were also asked whether they detected any differences in the attitudes or performance of shareholders and non-shareholders. One branch manager summed up a popular view: 'There is no difference at this depot between the effort levels of shareholders and non-shareholders, because the shareholders have dragged up the effort levels of non-shareholders.' This observation suggests the influence of horizontal monitoring, that is, employee-shareholders helped and encouraged other workers to work harder because they felt their stake would be affected by the effort of others. Another branch manager perceived the situation at his depot somewhat differently, with implications for improved industrial relations: 'It depends who's got the shares. In this depot the right people have got shares. The stewards and the people who have been with the company a long while are shareholders and they are the leading lights.' The same manager gave an example of how the 'leading lights' had facilitated good industrial relations since the buyout. Shop stewards had encouraged increased flexibility among colleagues. They had also agreed to temporarily drop a union rule that no 'agency drivers' should be contracted in order to secure a particular contract. The manager was certain that there was greater 'liaising' and 'cooperation' between himself and the shareholder shop stewards since the buyout.

Among the workforce, interviewees' perceptions of changes since the buyout were far less positive in general, with relatively slight differences between shareholders and non-shareholders. One fitter summarised the changes in the following way: 'We had a much better deal under nationalisation. We'd get more things for the workshop. But now it's so tight you've got to beg for everything.' But a fitter at another depot saw things quite differently: 'We're getting more and better contracts. We've got rid of those [workers] who sit in the canteen. Everyone is more flexible now. The takeover has brought in flexibility.' (Overall, however, manual employees gave the general impression that management had tried to improve flexibility, but it had been resisted.)

Respondents were also asked about their own effort levels and those of their colleagues. Thirty-four per cent of those who had been with BRS (Southern) before February 1982 said they had become more cost conscious since the buyout. Only 23 per cent felt that their colleagues worked harder since the buyout, although over 30 per cent answered that they did not know. Seventy-one per cent of interviewees did not see any differences between the performance of shareholders and non-shareholders. One driver commented that 'the ones who are not shareholders work hardest', though there does not appear to be any *a priori* reason for this suggestion. A clerical employee did observe a clear difference in the level of interest and perceived that 'shareholders do work a little harder'. The full benefits of having employee-shareholders were not being reaped, she added, because 'it is difficult to gee-up their workmates who drive all day on their own'. It is possible that the performance of both shareholders and non-shareholders had improved, but for different reasons. A non-shareholder driver remarked that 'they [the shareholders] are working harder to make profits, we're working harder to keep our jobs'.

Questionnaire survey findings

For a clearer picture, we turn to findings from the questionnaire survey, which investigated the effects of share ownership on employee attitudes and industrial relations in a more systematic way. The two hypotheses relating to the effects of ownership each generate four propositions, which are now examined more closely.

Share ownership generates disharmony

The first hypothesis is that a conversion to employee ownership will lead to new tensions at the workplace and less harmonious industrial relations. Four specific propositions are suggested:

Proposition 1: *Pressure on wages and unions*
A conversion to employee ownership places a constraint on wage increases which may lead to tensions between shareholders and non-shareholders.

Proposition 2: *Successful conversions*
(i) A 'successful' conversion creates resentment among non-participants, and (ii) an 'unsuccessful' conversion leads to new pressures on non-participants.

Proposition 3: *Differential rights*
Employee ownership leads to two-tier rights at the workplace which may create new disharmony.

Proposition 4: *Increased expectations of participation*
Employee ownership raises employee expectations of increased participation in decision-making.

Proposition 1: Pressure on wages and unions

Bradley and Gelb (1983a) recorded a decline in trade union bargaining power in employee buyout conversions outside the United States. At Manuest, a French furniture factory bought out by its employees in 1975, union density fell from 95 to 40 per cent during the conversion period. A diminished union role was also recorded at Scottish News Enterprises, Meriden Motorcycle Cooperative, Kirby Manufacturing and Engineering Company Ltd and Tembec. Stern (1982) suggested that, in some cases, support for the union may be sustained following conversion, but production workers may give preference to shareholder decisions in policy matters which suggests a weakening of the union in the long run.

The trade union's decline after an employee buyout is by no means inevitable.[5] At Byers Transport Limited, the trade union's fear of role loss after a conversion was unfounded (Long, 1979). Most employees, both unionised and non-unionised, did not think that unionisation was either incompatible with employee ownership or unnecessary. Long's data complemented anecdotal evidence from most unionised conversions in the United States where it seems the union has continued to perform similar functions and responsibilities. Strong trade union demands for worker rights may maintain the union's representative role.[6]

At the NFC, the new structure of ownership undoubtedly put pressure on the trade unions, particularly the TGWU. The dramatic growth in share value may to some extent justify the TGWU's allegation that the sale was a 'rip-off of the people's assets', but it also makes it impractical for the union to continue advising their members not to invest. Given the potential hostility that might be created towards the union, the

TGWU has switched its attention away from opposing the buyout to consolidating the existing collective bargaining and consultation practices and ensuring the wage awards are unaffected. To this extent the buyout does not appear to have affected the role of the trade unions and may have made them more efficient. The same machinery is still used and the closed shop has remained. If anything, trade union effectiveness has been tempered by the general change in the climate of industrial relations, and employee share ownership has supported this climate. According to Sir Peter Thompson:

> We still negotiate wages with trade unions; we still have got a theoretical closed shop in most of the companies. Fortunately, at the time we did the deal, they [the trade unions] were interested in devolving the negotiations away from the centre into the operating companies and that we did. So the great monolith which was the senior trade union officials talking with the directors of NFC has gone. (Interview between the authors and Sir Peter Thompson, December 1987)

Interviews with regional trade union officials and shop stewards suggest that increased pressure has been applied by management in pay negotiations to limit wage increases. But the union negotiators 'haven't let them get away with it'. A shop steward remarked that 'they [the management] tried to increase flexibility, but we weren't having any of it. They've still got to abide by the rules of the union.' Asked whether they thought wage rises had been kept down since the buyout in order to pay better dividends, some 53 per cent of the sample said they did, whereas 31 per cent did not and 16 per cent said they did not know. Among manual employees, some 56 per cent perceived that there had been pressure on wages, 24 per cent did not and 20 per cent did not know. Responses of shareholders and non-shareholders were then considered, but the differences were small for both the whole pre-buyout sample and the manual employees sub-sample, and statistical significance was not achieved. This would seem to suggest that some effort had been made to restrain wage rises, but that it was not a major source of tension. The unions also perceived an advantage in decentralised pay bargaining since it was difficult to exert influence over such a large and diffuse organisation as the NFC. At the local level unions believed they could be more effective. But Sir Peter Thompson also views decentralisation as an advantage: 'discussions about pay have become more pertinent'; NFC companies have 'become higher earning, more efficient and more productive businesses'.

Changes in the level of industrial action seem to have been minimal. Industrial militancy in the 1970s tended to be sporadic and to be confined to a local level, while the national machinery proved highly efficient.[7] The NFC's main industrial relations problem in the 1970s related to the overmanning in the parcels division which required redundancies. Despite the potential rivalry between the unions, redundancies were completed with little industrial disruption.

On the other hand, the incomes policy in the late 1970s did create labour relations tensions. In 1978 increases in management and clerical grades remuneration were kept within the government's 5 per cent guidelines, whilst manual employees, following arbitration, achieved an increase in line with the private sector. Consequently, membership of the Transport Salaried Staff Association (TSSA) increased dramatically. At BRS (Southern) membership of the TSSA increased by 64 per cent in 1979–80. It seems plausible that manual employees' pay rises were cushioned during this period by public sector status. The NFC's feeling was that the incomes policy had created rigidities in the pay structure compared to the flexibility of free collective bargaining.

There has been little industrial action at the NFC since the buyout. When it has occurred, it has been concentrated primarily in the parcel activities, where redundancies continued, and in depots with a high concentration of TGWU members. At BRS (Southern) where there have been difficult industrial relations in some locations in the past, the post-buyout record reflects the fact that the company has grown whilst including major pockets of TGWU strength. Minor disputes have reportedly taken place in depots in the London region in buoyant local labour markets and where the TGWU is most active. Overall, however, industrial disruption has not been a major problem.

Proposition 2: Successful conversions

Up to the time of the survey, the NFC's share prices had been rising and regular dividends were being paid. Similarly, the subsidiary BRS (Southern) was profitable and growing. Therefore, the buyout is classified as a success. Part (ii) of Proposition 2 is ignored as the need to improve performance and effort levels was not exigent.

Respondents were asked how successful the buyout at the NFC had been. Some 66 per cent said the buyout had been successful. Only 8 per cent perceived that it had been unsuccessful. A notable 26 per cent did not know. The responses of shareholders and non-shareholders were different (Table 7.1). Some 93 per cent of shareholders perceived the buyout to have been a success, compared with 43 per cent of non-shareholders.

It is perhaps unsurprising that so many employee-shareholders should judge the buyout a success, given the substantial financial gains made since

Table 7.1. *Perceptions of the buyout's success and employee ownership*

	Shareholders %	Non-shareholders %	Sample %	
Successful buyout				
Yes	92.8	43.4	65.8 (n	= 100)
No	2.9	12.0	7.9 (n	= 12)
Don't know	4.3	44.6	26.3 (n	= 40)
Total	45.4	54.6	100.0 (n	= 152)

Chi-square = 41.133, significant at less than 0.001 with 2 degrees of freedom.

Table 7.2. *Perceptions of the buyout's success and manual employee ownership*

	Shareholders %	Non-shareholders %	Sample %	
Successful buyout				
Yes	85.2	42.2	54.9 (n	= 50)
No	3.7	15.6	12.1 (n	= 11)
Don't know	11.1	42.2	33.0 (n	= 30)
Total	29.7	70.3	100.0 (n	= 91)

Chi-square = 14.185, significant at less than 0.001 with 2 degrees of freedom.

February 1982. The significant difference between employee-shareholders and non-shareholders does not necessarily suggest a potential source of tension. Tables 7.1 and 7.2 show that only 12 per cent of all non-shareholders and 16 per cent of manual employee non-shareholders perceived that the buyout had actually been a failure. A remarkable 45 per cent of non-shareholders said that they did not know whether the buyout had been a success or not, including 42 per cent of manual non-shareholders. It therefore seems likely that tensions have been avoided by an informational asymmetry following the buyout as well as before it.

Proposition 3: Differential rights

Following a conversion to employee ownership, shareholders may have certain privileges not enjoyed by non-shareholders. This has certainly been the experience in several American employee-owned firms, for example, the scavenger cooperatives, which employ some non-membership labour. Non-members tend to get the less desired jobs and are excluded from the

Table 7.3. *Perceptions of job security and employee ownership*[a]

	Shareholders %	Non-shareholders %	Sample %
Job security			
More secure	35.1	7.3	21.4 (n = 24)
Same	45.6	54.5	50.0 (n = 56)
Less secure	19.3	38.2	28.6 (n = 32)
Total	50.9	49.1	100.0 (n = 112)
Chi-square = 14.046, significant at 0.001 with 2 degrees of freedom.			

[a] Pre-buyout sub-sample.

decision-making process; their top wages are less than 70 per cent of the pay of most partners.[8]

The NFC's management has carefully eschewed creating such a two-tier system of employee rights. Share ownership is kept confidential so that officially nobody in the company outside the share trust knows who owns shares and who does not. Loan offers and wider share ownership campaigns have encouraged new employees to invest. Redundancies have been made regardless of shareholder status, so that in some sections shareholders have been made redundant, although they have of course been permitted to retain their shareholdings.

The question of differential rights was explored in the attitude survey. Sixty-seven per cent of respondents who joined the NFC before 1982 said the buyout had not created new divisions in the workforce in this respect, whereas 26 per cent perceived it had. Furthermore, 69 per cent of manual employees said that new divisions had not been created. Comparing responses of shareholders and non-shareholders, no statistically significant differences emerged. Apparently management has been reasonably successful in preventing the development of a cleavage in the workforce.

Respondents were asked if they felt their jobs had become more or less secure since the buyout. Just as the interviews had suggested that few felt the buyout had made much difference in this respect, 50 per cent of survey respondents perceived no change at all in job security, including 47 per cent of manual employees and 55 per cent of non-shareholders. However, some 35 per cent of shareholders perceived that their job security had increased compared with only 7 per cent of non-shareholders (Table 7.3). Among non-shareholders 38 per cent perceived a decrease in their job security, compared with 19 per cent of shareholders. Furthermore, 44 per cent of manual non-shareholders felt less secure (Table 7.4). These differences were statistically significant in chi-square tests at the 0.01 level.

Meaningful interpretation is not straightforward, however. Perceptions

120

Table 7.4. *Perceptions of job security and employee ownership: manual employees only*[a]

	Shareholders %	Non-shareholders %	Sample %
Job security			
More secure	34.8	6.7	16.2 (n = 11)
Same	43.5	48.9	47.0 (n = 32)
Less secure	21.7	44.4	36.8 (n = 25)
Total	33.9	66.1	100.0 (n = 68)
Chi-square = 9.667, significant at 0.01 with 2 degrees of freedom.			

[a] Pre-buyout sub-sample.

of job security may be more influenced by perceptions of management strategy than by perceptions of a bias against non-shareholders. One driver commented: 'I feel my job is much less secure now. All these depots have got to make money or they'll be shut. We're losing money because of bad management.' Nevertheless, it is worth noting that non-shareholders were twice as likely as shareholders to see the buyout as affecting job security.

Proposition 3: Two-tier rights

Survey data did not suggest that the buyout had created a two-tier system of employee rights. Respondents were asked some general questions relating to workplace relations and the company which attempted to measure differences between shareholders and non-shareholders in perceptions about treatment of workers. Over 65 per cent of all respondents perceived workplace relations as either 'good' or 'very good', including 60 per cent of respondents who had joined the company before the buyout, and 56 per cent of manual employees. Differences between shareholders and non-shareholders were insignificant in all tests. Furthermore, over 68 per cent of all employees said the company treated all its employees fairly, including 69 per cent of buyout respondents and 63 per cent of manual employees. Once again, statistically significant differences did not emerge between shareholders and non-shareholders. Finally, 42 per cent perceived no social division between managers and rank and file employees at their workplaces, compared to 50 per cent who did. The figures for manual employees were only marginally different. Nor were there significant differences between shareholders and non-shareholders.

Proposition 4: Increased expectations of participation

The effects of individual share ownership are frequently confounded by the effects of increased participation in decision-making which may accompany a change in ownership (Goldstein, 1978; Johannesen, 1979; Long, 1978b). Earlier studies have suggested that the benefits of increased participation in decision-making may be greater than those of becoming individual shareholders. The best outcome, however, would result if the two effects occurred together.

In some cases, employee ownership without an accompanying increase in participation appears to lead to increased conflicts and finally a reversion to conventional ownership (Johannesen, 1979; Bradley and Gelb, 1985). At Hyatt Clark Industries Inc., an employee buyout from General Motors in 1981, an initial period of modest profits was followed by labour troubles reflecting workers' frustration at their lack of influence (Bradley and Gelb, 1985). Lack of participation has also been evoked to explain the strike at South Bend Lathe in 1980 (Tannenbaum and Conte, 1976). Long's (1981) longitudinal survey suggests a decline in motivation over time as industrial relations deteriorated, in part because employee expectations of increased participation in decision-making had not been met. Workers were particularly frustrated by their inability to influence decisions directly relevant to the individual and his job. However, if participatory expectations are not raised during the transition period, then it seems plausible that a conversion to employee ownership need not be accompanied by new mechanisms for participation and will not lead to new tensions.

Senior management at the NFC have spoken of the increased participation of the workforce since the buyout. However, the company's mode of operation reflects a fundamental distinction between participation as owners (exercising ownership rights and obligations) and participation as employees (exercising control rights derived from belonging to a firm). The NFC has used communications to increase the first kind of participation. Three main methods are employed for communicating with shareholders. Firstly, quarterly regional meetings which are attended by a director provide information and enable the Board to receive some feedback from the grass roots. Between 50 and 100 shareholders normally attend. The issues discussed are minuted and reported back to the Board for discussion. Secondly, quarterly shareholder newsletters offer a forum for questions and accountability. Newsletters are sent directly to shareholders rather than circulated at the workplace. Thirdly, the annual general meetings (AGMs) of the consortium provide the only formal opportunity to employee-shareholders for actual control over decision-making. Decisions relating to the consortium are taken. Moreover, shareholders have the right to refuse the reappointment of directors and can voice criticism of operational management, corporate strategy, and so on.

Communication to employees as employees has also improved somewhat. The consortium has spent considerable sums of money in training management to accept and promote a participative style of management. Special information sheets, prepared by the NFC, keep non-shareholders informed about the company's performance, the opportunity to purchase shares, and so on. In addition, the NFC produces a monthly circular for managers, and some of the operating units produce their own company newsletters and information sheets.

Overall, these innovations appear to have met expectations satisfactorily. Interviews revealed some exceptions. A fitter who bought shares in February 1982 said that 'things have got worse. Management is bad; advertising is awful. There's little communication with the workers. Anything they [management] do tell is not volunteered information.' But these views contrasted strongly with the high attendance at the annual general meetings, on average some 2,000 shareholders, 8 per cent of the total workforce, have attended. This is a significant figure given that the NFC is a national organisation spread throughout Britain. In addition, the regional meetings and newsletters are regarded as successful by both senior management and rank and file workers.

Senior management also voiced some qualifications about the success in communications. Fear was expressed that two groups were being created in the organisation.[9] Communication with non-shareholder employees was often poor. The old trade union channels for information and consultation remained the only method for communicating in some areas, a source of potential disharmony.

Employees had never been led to expect increased participation in decision-making on a day-to-day basis, and the institutions for participation in decision-making have not changed at the operational level. Indeed, the Prospectus which invited employees to participate in the buyout had specified quite clearly that a conventional management structure would be retained in the event of a buyout conversion. This policy seems to mirror employee-shareholders' own desires. For example, after discussions about whether to appoint a shareholder or employee director, the shareholder director option was chosen, apparently reflecting the feeling that any control rights should be based upon ownership rather than employment. Therefore, it is unlikely that any expectations of increased participation in decision-making were in any way generated, other than the expectations of standard shareholder participation, and these appear to have been satisfied.

Employee share ownership and harmonisation of industrial relations

The previous section suggests that it is possible to avoid generating new tensions in the workforce with the introduction of employee ownership. But are there any positive, beneficial consequences of individual employee ownership?

Four specific propositions were examined more closely in the questionnaire survey:

Proposition 1: *Incentives and employee ownership*
(i) Employee share ownership reduces perceptions of the difference between the individual's interest and the company's objectives, and (ii) the individual shareholder perceives a closer link between his efforts, company performance and individual rewards.

Proposition 2: *Self-monitoring*
Individual self-monitoring increases, as a result of becoming a shareholder.

Proposition 3: *Horizontal monitoring*
Share ownership encourages employee-shareholders to help their colleagues to work harder and be more cost conscious.

Proposition 4: *Vertical monitoring*
Management-shareholders will make increased demands upon employees to work harder and be more cost conscious.

Proposition 1: Incentives and employee share ownership

The fragmented nature of the NFC organisation and its decentralised management structure have resulted in local depots being accounted as profit centres. This arrangement probably makes employee buyouts more feasible and, from our point of view, has the advantage of focusing individual efforts. Some 60 per cent of respondents from the questionnaire survey at BRS (Southern) saw themselves as primarily affiliated with their depots, rather than with BRS (Southern), the NFC or a client company. Furthermore, 58 per cent of respondents obtained more personal satisfaction from the depot's success than from the company's success.

In response to the question whether share ownership was an incentive for employees to take more interest in the company and be more cooperative, some 64 per cent of the questionnaire sample (and a similar proportion of the sub-sample which had joined the company before the buyout) perceived that it was. Among manual employees who had joined the company before the buyout, only 48.5 per cent perceived this incentive. More striking perhaps were the highly significant differences between shareholders and non-shareholders. Incentive effects were perceived by 85

Table 7.5. *Employee ownership and perceptions of incentives*[a]

	Shareholders (n = 69) mean	Non-shareholders (n = 83) mean	Significance[b]
Whole sample (n = 152) Share ownership			
Incentive to cooperate	2.130	2.964	$p < 0.001$
Incentive to increase efficiency	2.304	3.325	$p < 0.001$
Satisfaction from company success	1.913	2.651	$p < 0.001$
	Shareholders (m = 57) mean	Non-shareholders (n = 55) mean	Significance[b]
Pre-buyout sample (n = 112) Share ownership			
Incentive to cooperate	2.211	3.091	$p < 0.001$
Incentive to increase efficiency	2.386	3.618	$p < 0.001$
Satisfaction from company success	1.930	2.745	$p < 0.001$
	Shareholders (n = 27) mean	Non-shareholders (n = 64) mean	Significance[b]
Manual employees (n = 91) Share ownership			
Incentive to cooperate	2.259	2.938	$p < 0.05$
Incentive to increase efficiency	2.407	3.297	$p < 0.001$
Satisfaction from company success	2.037	2.688	$p < 0.05$
	Shareholders (n = 23) mean	Non-shareholders (n = 45) mean	Significance[b]
Pre-buyout manual employees (n = 68)			
Incentive to cooperate	2.391	3.133	$p < 0.05$
Incentive to increase efficiency	2.522	3.600	$p < 0.001$
Satisfaction from company success	2.087	2.822	$p < 0.05$

[a] The values shown in the table are mean scores on a Likert scale ranging from 1 (Great extent) to 5 (Not at all). Note 10 explains Likert scale employed and significance of means.

[b] Indicates the statistical significance in the differences in means in pooled t tests.

Table 7.6. *Employee ownership and increased cost consciousness*[a]

	Shareholders %	Non-shareholders %	Sample %
Increased cost consciousness			
Yes	77.1	41.8	59.8 (n = 67)
Unsure	1.8	10.9	6.3 (n = 7)
No	21.1	47.3	33.9 (n = 38)
Total	50.9	49.1	100.0 (n = 112)
Chi-square = 15.281, significant at 0.001 with 2 degrees of freedom.			

[a] Pre-buyout sub-sample.

per cent of employee-shareholders. In Table 7.5, every set of responses suggests a clear and strong association between share ownership and the incentive among employees to cooperate with management's objectives.[10]

Similarly, over 53 per cent of all respondents perceive share ownership offers an incentive to work more efficiently, although 42 per cent do not. Among employees who joined the NFC before the buyout, 45.5 per cent see no such incentive. Some 50 per cent of all manual employees, and 56 per cent of manual employees who joined before the buyout, see little or no incentive in share ownership. Table 7.5 shows the overall means for the incentives to improve efficiency are lower than for increasing cooperation. Once again, there were highly significant differences between shareholders and non-shareholders; 77 per cent of employee-shareholders feel that shareholding creates incentives to work more efficiently.

Using the same scale, respondents were also asked whether they gained personal satisfaction from the company's success. Seventy-one per cent said they did, including 70 per cent of the pre-buyout sub-sample. Among manual employees, 68 per cent gained some personal satisfaction; that proportion declined to 63 per cent for those who joined the company before the change in ownership. But of more interest were the strong differences between shareholders and non-shareholders.

Proposition 2: Self-monitoring

Given that employees seem to feel that share ownership creates incentives for cooperation and work effort, one might expect to find that individual self-monitoring improves as a result of becoming a shareholder. Previous studies are ambiguous about whether the motivation of employee-share-holders and non-shareholders differs. It seems plausible that favourable work-group norms may be created which improve the motivation of shareholders directly and subsequently raise the motivation of non-share-holders.

Some 60 per cent of the questionnaire sample said that they had become more cost conscious since the buyout. More striking is the difference between shareholders and non-shareholders. As Table 7.6 shows, 77 per cent of shareholders perceived they had become more cost conscious since the buyout, compared with 42 per cent of non-shareholders. The differences were highly significant. Similar results emerge for manual employees, suggesting that the positive effects of share ownership on individual self-monitoring are likely to extend to the whole firm. This result to some extent contradicts the findings of proposition 1, which suggest that the incentives may decline marginally among manual employees. Evidently cost consciousness is distinct from increased effort, although the difference cannot be quantified here.

Proposition 3: Horizontal monitoring

If employees increase their horizontal supervision as a result of becoming shareholders, such a change in work behaviour could have an important impact upon a firm. All respondents were asked whether they considered share ownership an incentive to encourage fellow employees to work harder and be more cost conscious. The overall response suggested there was potential for horizontal supervision and that it had been partially fulfilled at the NFC. Some 20 per cent of employees (and 42 per cent of shareholders) perceived share ownership as an incentive to encourage fellow employees. However, 58 per cent of shareholders saw no incentive to encourage others. When managers were removed from the sample (since they are likely to see such monitoring as part of their normal duties), results were not dissimilar. Some 16 per cent of non-managers and 16.5 per cent of manual employees perceived share ownership as an incentive to encourage fellow employees. Chi-square tests revealed statistically significant differences between shareholders and non-shareholders, suggesting that the potential for a greater increase in horizontal monitoring existed.

Why was this potential not realised more fully? One reason may be the relatively low percentage of shareholders at BRS (Southern) (compared with other units in the NFC) which may have led employees to keep their share ownership private rather than use it to influence colleagues. It also seems likely that a high proportion of non-management shareholders is needed to generate a high level of horizontal pressure. Findings from the plywood cooperatives in the United States (Bellas, 1972) and from Tannenbaum and Conte's (1976) survey have both shown an association between the proportion of the non-management workforce who own shares and the effects of employee ownership. Evidence from the NFC suggests a high level of horizontal pressure exists in groups of external contract drivers dominated by employee-shareholders and based at the client's facilities. Furthermore, lorry drivers tend to be independent, individualistic workers who are notoriously difficult to monitor (see Hollowell, 1968). The fact that they often spend much of their working day outside the depots reduces the potential for horizontal monitoring.

Finally, it is possible that as BRS (Southern) is currently profitable and growing, the NFC's share price is rising dramatically and regular dividends are being paid, the need to improve performance levels is not exigent. Horizontal pressure may increase if profits start to fall. In the view of Bradley and Gelb (1983a), some of the predicted improvements in industrial relations and horizontal control may not be realised without a crisis, or employee perceptions of a crisis.

Proposition 4: Vertical monitoring

Will management shareholders, who are in a better occupational position than others to bring efforts and rewards closer, increase their supervision of subordinates after a buyout? Managers interviewed at BRS (Southern) felt that their supervision of employees had not changed. (To report an increase would have implied they had not given their full efforts before.) Managers who did acknowledge improving their vertical monitoring attributed the change to the increased demands of being privatised in competitive markets and the increased volume of business. For example, one said, 'at Head Office we are working harder, but that is because our work-load has increased and the staff levels have stayed the same'. At the operational level, a similar view was expressed by a branch manager. 'Everyone is working harder, not because of the buyout but because of increased volume.' In addition, non-managerial employees mentioned changes in management demands upon them. One clerical worker said, 'there are more managers around now. There's been no change in workers' attitudes but managers are more motivated. Previously the government paid the bills, now they're looking for waste.'

In the questionnaire survey 67 per cent of respondents perceived that management had become more cost conscious since the buyout, including 63 per cent of non-management respondents. Respondents were also asked whether management made more demands upon employees following the buyout. Some 64 per cent of respondents who had joined before the buyout (including managers) perceived increased demands upon employees by management. When managers were excluded from the sample, over 66 per cent felt management demands had increased. But differences did not emerge between shareholders and non-shareholders for any sub-sample, suggesting a broad increase in vertical monitoring.

Finally, the questionnaire survey attempted to test whether shareholders' attitudes were related to the amount they had invested. Estrin, Jones and Svejnar's (1984) survey of European cooperatives attempted to relate internal characteristics of producer cooperatives to productivity levels. In some sub-samples, the average values of individual shares and loans were both positively related to productivity levels. On the other hand, Hammer and Stern (1980) found the amount invested to be less important. Questionnaire survey data from the NFC provided no evidence of a relationship between the amount invested and attitudes, which supports Hammer and Stern's (1980) proposition that the act of buying shares is psychologically more influential than the amount invested.

Summary of findings and conclusions

The two hypotheses which seek to explain the effects of employee share ownership upon industrial relations have been presented as mutually exclusive but in reality are to some extent compatible. It is plausible that a company which is divided into employee-shareholders and non-shareholders may generate positive outcomes from share ownership so long as potential resentments and tensions do not become overt. The questionnaire survey suggests that at the NFC, positive outcomes had been combined with skilful management to avoid the development of tensions.

Some pressure appears to have been placed on wages since the buyout, but it does not seem to have been a source of disharmony between shareholders and non-shareholders. Management's avoidance of a structure of differential rights for shareholders and non-shareholders, and the care taken not to raise hopes of greater participation in decision-making, appear to have been successful. Furthermore, although shareholders were more likely than non-shareholders to regard the buyout as a success, that difference in views does not seem to have built up resentments among non-shareholders.

The overall findings suggest that employee ownership does have the potential to harmonise industrial relations. Perceptions of the incentives of employee share ownership are clearly related to whether an individual owns shares or not. Moreover, this perception exists at all levels in the organisation with only marginal and statistically insignificant declines among manual employees. Shareholders also appeared to gain significantly more personal satisfaction from the company's success.

There also appears to be a clear association between employee share ownership and increased self-monitoring, with some difference between the potential for increased interest and cooperation, and for increased efficiency. Horizontal monitoring also appears to have increased somewhat since the buyout. Moreover, it appears that management monitoring, at both company and shop-floor level, has improved since the change of ownership. The similarity of perception between shareholders and non-shareholders suggests that potential tensions are unlikely to emerge as a result.

Although these findings support the hypothesis that employee share ownership can harmonise industrial relations, some qualifications are in order. Firstly, the data is cross-sectional, so causality should not be inferred. Nevertheless, the study has made a small step forward on this question. One cannot know whether attitudes relating to general perceptions of the incentives of employee share ownership, or the conduct of industrial relations in the firm, were formed before or after a decision to invest.

Secondly, the potential for still greater horizontal monitoring was suggested in the statistically significant differences between shareholders and non-shareholders and by some 20 per cent of the sample who perceived share ownership as an incentive to encourage horizontal monitoring. Bradley and Gelb (1983b) showed that horizontal control in the Mondragon cooperatives in Spain substantially reduces supervision and production control costs. The findings at the NFC suggest that horizontal control is to some extent related to work methods and technology. These factors are of course beyond the control of the firm. But the findings also suggest that to achieve a very large improvement in horizontal control, a high proportion of the manual employee work group may have to be shareholders.

Postscript

Our privatisation was different from any of the others in the sense that we started with an impossibly loaded balance sheet. We deliberately chose to do this in order that we could buy the company and retain 83 per cent of the equity in the hands of the employees. We started life with £7.5 million equity, £130 million debt and a new concept of running a business.

When we came out of the public sector we were very defensive trying to reduce the level of our debt. During the first 18 months we concentrated entirely on debt reduction. This entailed a negative strategy of pulling together all our different operating units, making them share common premises and selling the vacated premises. This was a knee-jerk reaction to the scenario that 'we've got so much debt, we've got very little earnings we've got very little profit which barely covers the interest on the debt and we didn't know whether we were going to be successful'.

We began to realise that we had a highly motivated management, and to a lesser extent a motivated workforce. We also had a set of potential customers who actually were 'turned on' by our ownership whereas previously they were 'turned off' by it. We could say to chairmen of large companies, 'hand over your distribution and the people who will be working on your behalf actually have a stake in the company, they are committed and they are not likely to strike'. And so we found dozens of investment opportunities which presented us with a dilemma: did we start expanding the business and forget about debt or did we continue down the route of trying to reduce debt?

We realised that if we kept on going down the route of negative accounts employment would continue to drop and this was unacceptable to an employee-owned company. So we had to become a different company. We had to grow. So we started to become a marketing-led company: never mind about debt as long as we could get back-to-back deals with blue-chip companies then we could start raising money and growing. (Interview between authors and Sir Peter Thompson, December 1987)

Today the NFC employs some 29,000 workers, of whom 25,667 own shares in the company. At the annual general meeting in February 1988 shareholders overwhelmingly endorsed the Board's recommendation to seek a Stock Exchange quotation for its shares. The quantitative improvement in the NFC's performance since the conversion in February 1982 has been outstanding. For FY 1986–7 turnover was £911 million and gross operating profits were £64.5 million. Sales represented a 22 per cent increase on the previous year with growth outpacing inflation by 17 per cent. Initially, operating profits were composed largely of property sales which concealed rather lower trading profits. However, trading profits increased from £4.1 million in 1981–2 to £40 million in 1986–7. In addition, over the five years 1978 to 1982, the NFC sold £47 million in property, but invested £41 million in new property and facilities. Furthermore, although the profits from property outstripped trading profits in 1981–2, and were still over 50 per cent of total operating profits in 1982–3, between 1983 and

1985 profits from property sales represented only 15 per cent of total operating profits.

Not all the NFC's activities have been profitable, however. Following the buyout some consistently made losses, and problems of over-capacity and very competitive markets have continued. In attempts to reduce labour costs, redundancies were forced upon the parcels activities which worsened their immediate overall losses, but were expected to improve the balance sheet in the future. Progress was disappointing, however, and in early 1986 the parcels activities were merged under a new trading name, National Carriers-Roadline, with subsequent job losses in Roadline. The NFC have always attempted to re-employ redundant workers in other parts of the organisation. After the merger of parcels activities, the NFC set up a Re-development Bureau to relocate redundant Roadline employees, both with the NFC and in outside jobs.

Besides increasing its trading profits, the NFC has improved in other performance indicators. Despite the high gearing ratio and interest rates in the early 1980s repayments on the medium-term loans have been made on time; there was even an early repayment of £6 million in December 1982. The process of diversification has accelerated. New investments overseas have been made. In the domestic market, the trend in the industry towards the use of external, specialist hauliers rather than in-house haulage has meant an increased demand for specialist distribution services. The NFC has kept pace with the new demand by developing its own distribution services. Furthermore, in March 1985 the NFC acquired SPD, one of the major distribution enterprises in Britain. The NFC reorganised its own operational structure later in 1985 to introduce a new Distribution Group built around the acquired SPD network.

The successful performance of the NFC since February 1982 has been reflected in the rewards to shareholders. After accounting for splits, rights issues, and so on, the share price, as calculated by independent valuers, has increased dramatically. The equivalent value of an original £1 share had increased to £6 by June 1984, to £22 by March 1986 and to £74 by January 1989. Dividend payments on those £1 shares had amounted to 55p by August 1984 and over £1.50 by March 1986, net of tax. In February 1982 the NFC's total market capitalisation was £7.5 million. By October 1987 it had increased to some £419 million and by January 1989 it had increased to over £600 million.

The consortium has not escaped internal criticism. One manager described the capital growth as artificial. He suggested that the NFC was moving into business areas that it knew little about but which offered quick returns. This policy was pursued at the expense of the company's infrastructure.

The substantial improvement in the NFC's performance since 1982 is not entirely due to employee ownership or privatisation but reflects a number of changes made since the late 1970s. Corporate policy has attempted to make the NFC more commercially effective by increasing emphasis on performance success. Unprofitable sections of the business have been allowed to dwindle while the company concentrates the specialised, more profitable services. This process, which included rationalisation of the property portfolio, continued into the 1980s. In addition a policy of participative management was formally introduced in 1977. Managers were encouraged to disseminate information more freely and to utilise the local joint committees more effectively. In 1987 the systems for providing employees with regular up-to-date information about the NFC's business activity and performance, as it affected an employee's own location, were refined so that in almost all operational units employees are now briefed face-to-face, on a quarterly basis. These meetings supplemented long-established procedures for consultation and communication between management and employees.

In the early 1980s, the company introduced performance-related rewards for management grades linked to meeting profit targets. Over time these schemes have increased in number and have been extended to include white-collar workers of all grades, and blue-collar workers in some depots. Currently the NFC employs some 32,000 workers, yet its productivity continues to improve, with revenue per employee increasing to a level of £32,130 in FY 1986–7. The company attributes this productivity improvement to its performance-related incentive schemes. Further, wage negotiations have been decentralised to group and operational company levels. The objective is to achieve remuneration packages more appropriate to the needs of a particular operation.

Privatisation has contributed to improved performance since 1982. Major organisational changes were made at the NFC in the early months after the buyout. Firstly, the NFC was restructured to include more executive directors to replace the non-executive directors who dominated the Board under public ownership and whose role had been to balance the operational needs of the NFC with the needs of the public interest. Secondly, the operating subsidiaries were reorganised. Companies with common activities were grouped more closely whilst retaining individual trading names and operational management. This was intended to reduce overheads and improve the marketing thrust of the various activities. The new collaborations have included increased site-sharing. By the end of 1984 there were over 70 multi-company depots and sites. Continued organisational restructuring has pursued the same goal of improving marketing by grouping common activities. All the parcels activities, for example, have been integrated into one operating group.

Control of property assets was transferred from the operating subsidiaries to the Board of the NFC and vested in a newly formed Property Group. This was a highly significant reorganisation for a number of reasons. The immediate objectives of the new Property Group were to increase the quality and capital value of the portfolio of properties, to administer the properties efficiently, to develop suitable properties on behalf of the operating companies, to handle property development and sales, and to dispose of surplus property. The property portfolio of the NFC would therefore be organised much more efficiently, and utilised more fully. The transfer of control to the NFC also reduced the attraction of any subsidiary to aggressive corporate investors intent upon asset-stripping following a public flotation, and considerably reduced the likelihood of the NFC being dismantled. The formation of the Property Group, therefore, cemented the unity of the NFC as an organisation.

After February 1982 the NFC was released from the capitalisation constraint imposed upon most nationalised industries. It was subsequently free to borrow in the capital markets and to invest freely, which has facilitated overseas investment, the development of new services and major domestic acquisitions. In addition the pension fund obligations, which had been a major source of concern, were largely cleared by the government at the time of sale.

Structural changes in the nature of the NFC's business have also been taking place at the subsidiary BRS (Southern), generating other changes independent from the buyout. General haulage has steadily declined as a proportion of turnover and has been replaced by specialised distribution services. In the financial year 1980–1, BRS (Southern) suffered a commercial collapse which led to the closure of several depots and redundancies, but the subsidiary is now experiencing a period of growth. The new business has generated a greater need for marketing, quality and efficient service. This challenge has resulted in the recruitment of a marketing and sales team, more participative management and performance-based competition between BRS (Southern)'s depots 'in the pursuit of excellence'.

Clearly both long-term factors and privatisation have influenced NFC's success, and indeed BRS (Southern)'s, since February 1982. Even so, an additional contribution may have been made by the employee ownership structure. Individual employee share ownership has been bolstered by communications with shareholders. Since the change in ownership the NFC has emphasised good communications with employees as a way of enhancing shareholders' identification with the firm whilst also acting as a channel for employees' input into decision-making.

Employee share ownership at the NFC

A crucial question is whether the NFC's highly participatory culture and its high level of employee ownership will persist after flotation. The Board argued that flotation was necessary for access to equity capital to finance growth. Moreover, if employees wished to sell their shares but were unable to do so, because no internal buyers were available, a creeping flotation would result as shares filtered out to NFC's institutional investors at less than full price.

Before the 1988 annual general meeting the company commissioned a survey of employee attitudes towards flotation. Over 70 per cent of shareholders (weighted by size of holding) agreed that the NFC should seek a Stock Exchange quotation. But some 87 per cent of the same group also hoped the company would remain employee controlled. The company has taken certain safeguards to facilitate continued employee control. They have enshrined in their Articles the double voting rights for employee shareholders on the issue of a takeover bid for the NFC. Further, employees will continue to be encouraged to buy shares and assisted by interest-free loans. And if the Board decides it needs to raise additional equity, any new shares will be offered first to existing shareholders before outside finance is sought. However, since share value will probably rise some 15 to 20 per cent after flotation and most workers stand to make considerable capital gains, it is uncertain whether the NFC will remain controlled by its employees. According to Sir Peter Thompson, the Chairman:

> You've got to have confidence that the concept of employee
> control is deep enough that it will survive on the backs of
> people believing in it. If they don't believe in it now, then it
> goes. It is time to cast loose and let's see if the employees do
> believe in it.

8

Conclusions

We have examined the experience of a pioneering British employee-owned firm, the National Freight Consortium, in order to explore three research issues: (i) why do buyouts from the public sector occur? (ii) what determines the employee investment decision in buyout situations? and (iii) how does individual employee share ownership affect industrial relations?

Our study has provided some tentative answers. Firstly, it suggests that the situations in which management and employee buyouts occur are increasing. They are no longer confined to plant closures, as was the case in the early recorded buyouts from the private sector, but are now resulting from the sale of public enterprises. Privatisation is a complex phenomenon resulting from a combination of ideological, economic and political factors. The employee buyout at the NFC was a way of balancing the government's competing objectives in privatisation given the political constraints and the NFC's marketability problem in 1981. Indeed, from the perspective of public policy, buyouts offer the prospect of extending the privatisation of state enterprises into less desirable firms. By bringing these enterprises to a wider market through buyouts, privatisation comes closer to achieving its objectives of dispersing the ownership of industry more widely while contracting the role of the state.

Secondly, the changing nature of buyouts was reflected in the 'dependence' hypothesis. The employee investment decision at the NFC was motivated by a number of different mutually reinforcing factors which included fear of job loss and the desire to make capital gains. But survey evidence suggested that the informational asymmetry hypothesis developed in Chapter 4 fits better with the circumstances at the NFC. Employee investment was associated with a desire for capital gains and was contingent upon company information available to employees at the time. Managers, who had greater access to information, were more likely to invest than non-managers. Manual employees who received the Transport and General Workers' Union's recommendation not to invest were

136

the least likely to invest. The union's strength was found to be diluted somewhat in smaller locations, and the propensity to invest among manual employees was higher in these locations. Finally, there was an association between the decision to invest and home ownership which appears to support the government's policy objective to create a property-owning democracy.

Thirdly, we hypothesised that conversion to employee ownership might hurt industrial relations by creating a new division in the workforce (between shareholders and non-shareholders) or creating expectations from employee ownership that could not be met. The empirical evidence from the NFC suggests that the potential conflicts had been contained. In addition, there were indications that industrial relations had actually improved. Relationships emerged between employee share ownership and perceptions of the incentives of share ownership. The act of buying shares seemed to be more important than the amount of shares purchased. Employee share ownership was perceived to have a greater effect on 'cooperation' than on 'performance'. Although management shareholders appeared to be slightly more 'cooperative' than non-management share-holders, the differences were not statistically significant. The use of cross-sectional data made it difficult to determine whether employee share ownership caused the attitudinal differences in respondents. However, some support was found for the proposition that employee share owner-ship improves individual employees' cost consciousness. This area requires much more research.

Some caution should be employed since our attitudinal data was taken from one company within the NFC group. Despite this caveat the NFC's experience has shed some light on the three specific research issues we examined. It has also provided some public policy implications. Another question remains: what have we learned about broader questions relating to the changing political, economic and managerial environments and their impact upon industrial relations?

Recently changing patterns of labour and product markets have engen-dered major changes in traditional collective bargaining. The rationale for the traditional form of trade unionism was the prospect of extracting larger proportions of surplus through collective action. Without such a surplus, traditional forms of union behaviour make less sense. As sur-pluses have been squeezed in traditionally unionised sectors, union mem-bership has fallen; at the same time the fragmentation of large production units has increased the costs of organising. The nature of traditional collective bargaining has begun to be challenged. To a degree, institutions appear to evolve endogenously on the basis of their suitability to par-ticular problems, through a form of institutional Darwinism which increases the scope of some relative to others. This natural selection is now operating in the institutions of the labour market and will have a significant impact on the future pattern of collective bargaining and industrial organisations. There is likely to be: (i) a movement away from the broader labour collectives towards collectives organised at the firm level, and (ii) scope for more flexible employment contracts at the firm level. The NFC is at the cutting-edge of this development and therefore provides an important object-lesson in the effect of employee ownership on employee attitudes and a tentative pointer for the development of human resource management

Another question for future research which our study raises is concerned with the increasing willingness of financial institutions to become involved with buyout schemes, partly a function of the steady deregulation of the financial markets both internationally and in Britain. Deregulation has made the financial market more competitive while enabling the entry of foreign banks with different products into the British market. The nature of the relationship between financial institutions and corporate decision-making should therefore be explored more fully and become part of the calculus of employee relations. To widen the issue, what role do other corporate advisers play, directly or indirectly, in managements' organisation of labour? Do bankers, accountants, management consultants and lawyers play an important role in facilitating employee financial participation schemes? If so, what are their evaluations based on?

Like deregulation of the financial markets, privatisation of state enterprises reflects the renewed concern for competitiveness. The economic arguments for shifting ownership are simply stated: privatisation is expected to inject the renewed energy of market forces into the firms concerned. The pursuit of profit and growth will encourage firms to be more dynamic and innovative which will improve their efficiency, competitiveness and responsiveness to consumer demands.

Privatisation may also be viewed as a method of helping the labour market to adjust to the changed economic environment of the late twentieth century. The sale of those enterprises inflicts three fundamental direct shocks upon traditional public sector industrial relations. Firstly, by removing entrenched procedural collective bargaining arrangements, often embodied in nationalisation legislation, it gives management an opportunity to restructure industrial relations. Secondly, by exposing some newly privatised enterprises to market forces, it changes the environment in which substantive industrial relations issues are negotiated. Thirdly, by enriching the nature of employee financial interest through employee share schemes, wider share ownership and home ownership, privatisation encourages employee identification with capital. The consequences of these changes for industrial relations are only just beginning to be understood. Our findings from the NFC, for example, suggest that employee share ownership is likely to affect workforce orientations. The property-owning democracy in all its manifestations, including the increasingly complex nature of employee financial interests, is a challenge to, amongst other things, traditional trade union organisation and conventional industrial relations academics.

Many trade unions have resisted these developments. At the NFC, the TGWU campaigned against the buyout, which was completed successfully nevertheless. Such resistance may be a major obstacle to public policymakers' attempts to widen employee share ownership and profit-related pay. But there are indications of a change in the trade union approach. The formation of Unity Trust Bank plc, backed by the trade union movement, to encourage employee share ownership may represent a watershed in the changing attitude of organised labour. In addition, a new realism in industrial relations has been manifested in such phenomena as no-strike agreements (Bassett, 1986), flexible working, the spread of quality of working life programmes, company level joint consultation committees (Brown, 1981; Daniel and Millward, 1983; Millward and Stevens, 1986), the split in the TUC and the labour movement's re-evaluation of its role (*Financial Weekly*, 1986).

The importance of privatisation accompanied by employee shareholding, and employee financial participation in general, therefore becomes clear. The radical change in the structure of ownership presents a significant challenge to the parameters of industrial conflict. In this study we have examined a privatised firm with a radically different structure of ownership. Findings give support to the view that buyout conversions may be an effective way of reallocating ownership of public sector productive assets; they may also have important implications for traditional industrial relations and productive efficiency.

Notes

1 The emergence of employee ownership

1 Prior to nationalisation, as a result of the Transport Act 1980, the National Freight Corporation was changed from a public corporation to a limited company and renamed the National Freight Company Ltd.

2 A third approved scheme, the discretionary share option scheme introduced in the Finance Act 1984, has been even more successful. By January 1989 some 3,616 schemes had been approved. Since these schemes tend to be restricted to executives, however, they are outside the scope of this study.

3 The 5 per cent limit of profits is not one of the Inland Revenue's conditions for approval, but is recommended by the Investment Protection Committee of the British Insurance Association and National Association of Pension Funds. Their concern is to ensure that employee financial participation schemes do not dilute excessively a company's ordinary share capital. The committee's guidelines have been accepted by its patrons, the insurance companies, pension funds and other major investors. Any proposed scheme may therefore have to comply with the guidelines to secure the approval of these investors (Richardson and Nejad, 1986).

4 In addition to the share-based profit-sharing schemes, there are cash-based schemes, which may be preferred as having a more direct effect on workers, and lower administration costs (Lloyd, 1976). Until recently, there were no reliable data for the number of these schemes in operation. Smith (1986) showed that 6 per cent of firms in a survey of 1,125 had a cash-based scheme whereas 15 per cent had share-based schemes. In 1987 a new measure was introduced by the government to promote 'simple' profit-sharing: profit-related pay (PRP). Under an approved scheme, tax advantages were made available to private firms who give a profit-related bonus as part of the annual pay bill. Fifty per cent of the profit-related pay received by an employee up to a maximum of £3,000, or 20 per cent of total pay is exempt from income tax.

5 The discretionary share scheme under the Finance Act 1984 gives selected employees an option to buy the company's shares, which may be exercised between three and ten years after the option is granted provided that the maximum value of each employee's option is four times his annual salary or

£100,000, whichever is greater. Any capital gains are free of income tax liability.

6 An important exception is Baxi Partnership, the largest employee-owned manufacturing company in Britain. In 1983 the owners converted the firm to employee ownership with a combination of individual ownership and a majority shareholding in trust. The reasons for using a combination of individual and social ownership are discussed in Bradley and Gelb (1986: pp. 34–6).

7 For a summary of the operation of an Employee Stock Ownership Plan (ESOP) in the United States, see: Bradley and Gelb (1986) and Copeman et al. (1984).

8 For example, in autumn 1984 when British Telecom was privatised, three schemes were offered to employees. Firstly, a free offer was made of 54 shares. Secondly, for those employees who invested their own money, two shares were given for each one bought subject to a maximum of £300. Thirdly, a 10 per cent discount was available for any other shares bought, up to a maximum of £1,600. A similar set of schemes was offered to British Gas employees on privatisation in autumn 1986.

9 For a discussion of the influence of different cultural traditions upon the nature of employee ownership in Britain and the United States, see Bradley and Gelb (1983a: ch. 5).

10 In addition, the trust can make a small annual allocation to new employees who wish to invest.

11 This problem prompted the consortium to think about certain changes in structure to facilitate realisation in capital gains. The decision to float the company on the London Stock Exchange solves that problem.

2 Privatisation and employee ownership: issues

1 See, for example: Bluestone and Harrison, 1982; Bradley and Gelb, 1983a; Stern et al., 1979; Wright and Coyne, 1985.

2 The source of this data is *British Business*, 23 January 1981: p. 178 and 24 April 1986: p. 189.

3 A novel feature of the merger wave was the high level of conglomerate mergers everywhere. Corporations with high profits diversified to reduce the volatility of their returns, and to improve their market power (see, for example, George and Joll, 1981).

4 In 1983 nearly 50 per cent of British manufacturing industry was controlled by 40 firms with 30,000-plus employees. In the United States and France, the same measurements were 33 and 20 per cent respectively (Economist Intelligence Unit, 1984).

5 The demerger boom of the early 1980s gave way to a period of 'megamergers' in the mid-1980s in both Britain and the United States. The causes of this renewed merger activity lie beyond the scope of this study. From our perspective, it suggests that mergers may continue to fuel buyouts as corporations

divest unwanted parts of new acquisitions. 'In the normal course of business development the process of acquisition and diversification, and the equally important divestment and disintegration will produce a fluidity in the economy which we would expect to continue to generate buyout opportunities' (Wright and Coyne, 1985: p. 6).

6 In most of the buyout cases recorded by Bradley and Gelb (1983a), some public support was given. Where private investment also occurred, Bradley and Gelb identified three main sources outside the workforce: sympathy capital from those concerned about a friend's or family member's job loss; linked capital provided by those with a stake in the survival of the enterprise; and 'capital plus management', by which an entrepreneur made an investment in return for some control over day-to-day management.

7 The 'Benn' cooperatives are early examples of phoenix cooperatives (i.e. they rise from the ashes of redundant businesses). These rescues have been encouraged by the Co-operative Development Agency (CDA), set up in 1978 by an Act of Parliament. The CDA's role is primarily advisory, as it has no funds of its own with which to assist new ventures. It also publishes guidelines for those considering setting up producer cooperatives (Co-operative Development Agency, 1986).

8 The remaining 20 per cent resulted from vendors transferring ownership to the workforce on retirement. The proportion is high as these companies tend to be transferred in good health, and Wright and Coyne's (1985) survey only covered survivor buyouts. Retiring owners may wish to transfer ownership to the workforce or management for a number of reasons: (i) to avoid a succession problem in a family firm; (ii) to keep the company independent; and (iii) as a philanthropic gesture. The importance of this source of buyouts should not be underestimated. A recent study found that some 10 per cent of all bankruptcies and voluntary liquidations in France were the result of a succession problem in a family business (Job Ownership Ltd, 1986a). A management or employee buyout may therefore be viewed in some cases as 'une belle sortie'.

9 Sir Keith Joseph was a member of the Conservative government 1979–83 and a key advocate of privatisation (Riddell, 1983).

10 In a preface to a pamphlet on how to widen share ownership, Edward Du Cann (1984) put the case clearly: 'Business-ownership, home-ownership and share-ownership are the best anti-Marxist barriers of all.'

11 Another strand to this argument is the issue of 'implied shareholdings'. Public ownership impinges upon freedom by denying the individual 'his' stake in any public asset, and forcing him to hold an implied shareholding which he may not privately choose. Freedom is therefore increased by the sale of public sector assets, thereby allowing individuals to choose to hold a stake in any such assets. Heald and Steel (1982) noted the narrow definition of liberty implied by the arguments of libertarians which ignored social freedoms. Moreover, the implied shareholding arguments assumed that the allocation of investment funds through the operation of the capital markets was socially optimal. The social returns of maintaining a British steel industry may be higher than the private returns. Alternatively, Britten (1984) has argued that the optimal

allocation of ownership can be achieved by a general give-away of public assets to each citizen, although the feasibility of this option has been challenged (Pliatzky, 1985).

12 A 'natural monopoly' is defined as an industry in which a single firm can produce more efficiently than two or more firms *at any one level of output* (Vickers and Yarrow, 1985).

13 For a discussion of economies of scale in the road freight transport industry post-nationalisation, see Chapter 3. The concept of 'externalities' was developed in the 1960s (see, for example, Nove, 1973). It argues that private sector investment criteria do not consider external costs and benefits, both social and economic.

14 Pryke's (1971) study of the nationalised sector during 1958–68 concluded that the public enterprises had outperformed private enterprise. However, in a similar study of the period 1968–78, Pryke (1981) attributed the disappointing performance of the nationalised industries to their being in the public sector.

15 Yarrow's (1986) survey incorporated Pryke's (1982) comparative study of the peripheral activities of some British nationalised industries and their private competitors, namely electricity and gas showrooms, and Sealink ferry service, then owned by British Rail. Pryke's evidence was overwhelmingly in favour of private enterprise.

16 Ironically, both nationalisation and private enterprise may be feared for concentrating economic power in natural monopolies. 'If monopoly is really inevitable, it is a finely balanced question whether state or private monopoly is worse' (Brittan, 1984: p. 117).

17 For example, profits may be transferred to the Exchequer, or used to subsidise other parts of the same organisation. The full implications of cross-subsidisation are unclear. Moreover, any division of services into profitable and social (non-profitable) services, followed by the privatisation of profitable services, effectively ending cross-subsidisation, may reduce overall productive effeciency. It may also increase public expenditure (Heald, 1983).

18 For example, the Transport Act 1968 which set up the National Freight Corporation included detailed instructions to the new Board about the relationship with the Secretary of State.

19 Evidence suggests that capital markets may view 'hybrid' enterprises (those firms in which the government retains a large shareholding) as still underwritten by the government. Consequently they may be able to borrow at favourable rates (Steel, 1984).

20 The Labour Research Department (1983) claimed that reducing the PSBR by revenue from sales and the 'massaging' of accounting as permitted by convention, was one of the principal reasons for privatisation. But Brittan remarks that 'privatisation has of course at times come in handy for cosmetic PSBR purposes; but it is ludicrous to suppose that major industrial decisions such as whether to denationalise the telephone system or gas or electricity have been taken mainly to massage the PSBR figures' (1984: p. 113).

21 The publication of Peacock and Shaw (1981) coincided with a notable shift in the 1979–83 Conservative government's view of the aims of privatisation, as reflected in both the presentation of written information about asset sales and

the content of ministerial speeches, notably those of the Financial Secretary (Treasury, 1982; 1983; 1984; Moore, 1983; 1984). Greater attention was given to the benefits of privatisation to consumers and the effects on efficiency, whilst the implications for the PSBR were de-emphasised.

22 Between 1979 and 1985, defence expenditure increased 30 per cent in real terms. The government pledged to maintain expenditure on the health service, and has produced figures to suggest that between 1979 and 1985 real spending increased by 20 per cent (Treasury, 1986).

23 For example, between 1979 and 1985 expenditure on social security increased by 34 per cent.

24 The institutionalisation of industrial relations may also have mixed consequences. See Chapter 3 for the case of the road haulage industry.

25 Freeman and Medoff (1984) argued that the trade union's collective 'voice' allowed employees to influence industrial relations policies. In the market mechanism, by contrast, the primary signals to management are exit and entry. The collective voice therefore enabled workers to express discontent by means other than quitting.

26 Pay is by far the largest component of public expenditure, representing some 60 per cent of the total in 1972. Another strand of this argument emerged from a study of the relative earnings of public and private sector employees (Foster et al., 1984). The findings suggested that during 1972–83 earnings in the public corporations continuously remained ahead of the rest of the economy, including the rest of the public sector. Moreover, public corporations tended to lead on earnings rather than to be led.

27 The discussions of the 'secret' Conservative Party group on the nationalised industries were reported in the *Economist* (1978).

28 Other approaches to controlling public sector unions have also been attempted. After 1978, external financial limits (EFL) were imposed upon nationalised industries, but the trade unions circumvented this restraint by politicising negotiations over the 'cash limits' of the EFLs (Bevan, 1980). After 1979, the Conservative government adopted a range of measures including restrictive legislation, the decentralisation of collective bargaining, and privatisation.

29 Since the early 1980s, management or employee buyouts have begun to outnumber sales by conventional methods (Coyne and Wright, 1982b).

30 See Chapter 3 for a detailed post-war history of the road haulage industry.

31 The same contradiction exists in the government's commitment to sell council housing to tenants at heavily discounted prices, sometimes as much as 60 per cent below market value.

32 Some of the Conservative government's own supporters criticised the privatisation programme for these reasons. The late Earl of Stockton, for example, compared the privatisation programme to the sale of the 'family silver' (see for example: *The Times*, 9 November 1985).

3 Privatisation and employee ownership: the NFC conversion

1 The road freight transport, or road haulage industry, is taken to include all hauliers who carry for hire and reward, and excludes those carrying primarily their own goods.

2 Four executives were formed to run London Transport, British Railways, the Docks and Waterways, and Road Transport. The Road Transport Executive (RTE) initially had charge of provincial bus services as well as road haulage activities, but the former responsibility was removed in early 1949. The RTE was then renamed the Road Haulage Executive (RHE)

3 These were the general haulage firms holding 'A' and 'B' licences under the licensing system introduced in the Road and Rail Traffic Act 1933, who carried only for others for hire and reward, and half of whose business was haulage of traffic for over 40 miles. Private hauliers carrying their own goods under 'C' licences were left in the private sector.

4 The exceptions were long distance hauliers in specialised activities such as furniture removals, liquids in bulk, and meat.

5 British Transport Commission, 'Integration of Services by Road and Rail: A Statement of Policy', July 1950.

6 In general, depots did not sell very easily and vehicles were sold only in small batches. The bigger units, notably in parcels carrying and meat haulage, were particularly difficult to sell.

7 *Reorganization of the Nationalized Transport Undertakings*, Cmnd 1248, HMSO, 1960.

8 In addition, the new Transport Holding Company controlled Thomas Cook, parts of what later became the National Bus Company, and several shipping lines. In all, some 90 companies were involved with an initial capital of £122.5 million.

9 The NFC took over the Transport Holding Company's (THC) road haulage activities. The bus companies in the THC went into a National Bus Company which left the THC with travel interests, including Thomas Cook and Pickfords Travel Service. Thomas Cook was later transferred to British Rail, while Pickfords Travel Service was moved to the NFC. The companies which the NFC inherited continued to enjoy generous autonomy, but were organised into three operational groups: general haulage and container traffics; parcels; and special traffics. The old British Road Services continued trading as part of the general haulage and container traffics group.

10 The Transport Act 1968 replaced the three licence categories of the Road and Rail Traffic Act 1933 with two forms of licence. 'Quality' licensing was designed to achieve high standards of safety and service. 'Quantity' licensing was designed for improving the coordination of freight transport by road and rail. The scheme permitted road transport of bulk cargoes for any distance, and all normal haulage for any distance over 100 miles, only if the railways could not provide a suitable substitute. In addition, the 1968 Act reduced the maximum working day to 11 hours, or 60 hours a week with one full day's rest.

11 Although nationalisation of road freight was primarily related to transport integration, it was also expected to raise productive efficiency by creating economies of scale. BRS' larger depots arguably reduced the average costs of maintenance and repairs, and new vehicles could be bought at a cheaper 'fleet' rate. The larger operation also facilitated the introduction of mechanisation. But the single largest advantage BRS had over private hauliers, even after 1956

when denationalisation ended, was that it provided a national network. Consequently average costs in general haulage were reduced because there was a natural clearing house system to reduce 'empty running'. Some economists (for example, Chisholm, 1959) argued that as the average size of haulage firms in the private sector was growing in the 1950s, the development of an adequate clearing house system between private hauliers would have reduced diseconomies. In reality, such a level of cooperation was highly unlikely in road freight transport given the competitive nature of the industry.

As the sole supplier of a network service, BRS also enjoyed demand side advantages. After denationalisation, customers who required widespread distribution services were concerned that they might be unable to find private hauliers with the capacity to handle all their traffic at reasonable rates, or that they would be forced to use several different hauliers. Their concern helped forestall complete denationalisation. 'Surprising as it may seem, capitalist interests intervened to preserve public ownership' (Pryke, 1971: p. 30). The value of these size advantages to BRS is difficult to assess. However, the persistently high number of small operators in the industry suggests there is a 'natural' advantage of smallness. In particular, the increased size of operational units may have diminished the quality of service (Hart, 1953). The bureaucratic procedures of the large organisation tend to reduce flexibility, promptness and occasional rule-bending relating to the conditions of vehicles and drivers' hours.

12 The lower performance in the period 1948–58 can be explained largely by the initial organisational difficulties in nationalisation, followed by the problems of integration up to 1953, and then the effects of denationalisation.

13 From the Transport Development Group's Annual Report, 1967, which is cited in Thomson and Hunter (1973: pp. 251–2).

14 Reported in Thomson and Hunter (1973).

15 In the years after the formation of the NFC, consideration was given to a merger of National Carriers and Roadline which might have led to a rationalisation of the NFC's parcels activities. But the merger was never approved: the companies did different types of work; there would have been a loss of business; and the trade unions were opposed.

16 For example, the BRS group within the NFC diversified into distribution in 1973, and truck rental in 1975.

17 There were over 100,000 licensed road haulage operators in 1977. *Road Haulage Operators' Licensing:* Report of the Independent (Foster) Committee of Inquiry, HMSO, London, 1979.

18 Cited in McLachlan (1983: p. 87).

19 The NFC inherited the pensions problem in the Transport Act 1968. When the Corporaton acquired the British Railways subsidiaries, it also acquired pension fund obligations that proved to be a major financial burden during the 1970s. In 1978, when the NFC underwent capital reconstruction, the pension fund obligations were modified. The government agreed to fund the deficits for 'rail-based' employees, but not for 'road-based' employees. The complications increased because all employees were assimilated in the NFC's three pension

funds. Thus the NFC was left with a substantial pension fund burden. To make the NFC an attractive proposition for private investment – a major objective of the Transport Act 1980 – some solution had to be found to the remaining pension fund deficiencies. The 1980 Act adopted a four-way split. Road-based and rail-based groups' obligations were each divided into two sub-groups: the historical and non-historical. Historical obligations were those entered into before April 1975. The government decided it would give a once-and-for-all lump sum to cover the deficiencies on road-based historical liabilities. The rail-based historical obligations, however, would be met as they arose, month by month; that is they would be permanently financed.

Once the lump sum payment had been made, all future unfunded road-based liabilities would have to be paid by the newly formed National Freight Company, or its new owners, with two exceptions. Firstly, as the NFC's pension funds were index-linked, the government would make a contribution in line with increases granted to public sector pensioners. Secondly, if there was a shortfall in the pension funds arising from the non-historical part of the liabilities, the NFC would not be obliged to fund the shortfall. Instead, benefits could be readjusted unless it was agreed that either or both employers and employees should pay additional contributions. The 1980 Act did not state the amount to be given to finance the road-based historical obligations. This crucial fixed lump sum was to be determined at the time of the NFC's sale. It was estimated to be some £40 million.

20 The sale of British Transport Hotels during 1980 had been an example. The hotels were eventually sold individually or in groups after prolonged negotiations with bidders, evaluation of the best packages and often resistance from trade unions or the workforce.

21 Little information about this late bid is available, making it impossible to determine the reasons for its failure. It may be that after the buyout had been accepted by the government, consideration of any other offer, including potentially better bids, would have alienated the NFC's management, leading to obstructions or mass departures that would have reduced the attractiveness of the group.

22 The document was entitled 'Principles of a Management-Led Consortium'.

23 See McLachlan (1983: p. 74).

24 The five main trade unions at the NFC are the Transport and General Workers' Union (TGWU); the Transport Salaried Staff Association (TSSA); the National Union of Railwaymen (NUR); the Amalgamated Union of Engineering Workers (AUEW); and the United Road Transport Union (URTU).

25 The document produced by Schroders was entitled 'Introduction of Private Capital into the NFC'.

26 The NFC's low gross margins meant that the company had a high operational gearing. Therefore, a small change in the relationship between costs and income would have a disproportionate effect on profits. The NFC's high proportion of fixed costs, another gearing factor, meant that only small changes in income were reflected in profits. In addition, even if the pensions

funds deficiencies were covered by the government, Schroders considered that the NFC would be vulnerable in the future because the pensions funds were large in relation to the Group's equity capital and reserves. Finally, the cash limits on the nationalised industries had hampered the NFC's development, so a smaller debt burden for new NFC Ltd would increase its flexibility.

27 This last point was of crucial importance in the government's eventual response to trade union demands during consultation over the Transport Bill, and subsequently influenced the TGWU's position regarding the buyout. Meeting with the Secretary of State for Transport in September 1979, the five main trade unions at the NFC pressed the government to retain at least 50 per cent of the NFC and to safeguard employees' terms and conditions of employment after any sale. The secretary of state made no commitment on which method of sale would be employed and agreed to safeguard employees' terms and conditions only during the incorporation phase after the passage of the Transport Bill. Once the NFC was privatised, free collective bargaining would determine substantive and procedural matters relating to employees. In other words, no guarantees were made.

28 In August BMB were requested by the consortium to ask their parent if an alternative contingency option could be made available. Barclays Bank finally agreed to make an unsecured loan in the event of the failure of the Companies Bill, but in return for a much larger equity stake.

4 The employment investment decision: issues

1 For example, the Bullock Report (1977) focused on increasing employee institutional representation in the decision-making process rather than encouraging employee ownership. However, the re-evaluation now under way in some trade unions does not appear to rule out the possibility of worker shareholders. Indeed, trade unions through their financial support of the Unity Trust Bank implicitly support Employee Stock Ownership Plans. Further, the increase in individual shareholdings has forced the TUC and some of its constituent unions to address the issue of worker shareholders.

2 The experience was similar in the United States and Germany during the same period (Bendix, 1963; Poole, 1975).

3 See, for example, Trades Union Congress (1974).

4 This is also a factor in Quality of Working Life programmes, including quality circles (see, for example, Bradley and Hill, 1983 and 1987).

5 There is some dispute about the extent of the growth in private share ownership. Estimates are based on a series of market surveys conducted during 1986. A survey in February estimated that only some 8.3 per cent of the adult population owned shares while a National Opinion Poll survey of 7,200 adults commissioned by the Treasury estimated the figure to be closer to 14 per cent. An estimate of 16 per cent (September 1986) was based on a sample of 2,000 adults undertaken by the British Market Research Bureau (see *Financial Times*, 1986). Current estimates are around 19 per cent.

6 The trade unions' response is of course a function of various challenges. Between 1979 and 1986, trade union membership fell by some 20 per cent while union density declined steadily, from 55 per cent to below 45 per cent (Bradley and Gelb, 1986; Department of Employment, 1987). These changes have not been due solely to excess supply in the labour market engendered by recession or employment legislation. In 1985 union membership fell by 2.5 per cent despite a rise of 0.8 per cent in employment. Other changes in the private sector suggest the trend may be more permanent. For example, the British economy has been increasingly penetrated by multinational enterprises with a preference for non-unionised or 'cooperative' labour (Brown, 1981). In addition, technological change has displaced workers in manufacturing sectors considered to be trade union strongholds. For example, employment in engineering, chemicals and textiles fell by over 20 per cent between 1979 and 1985. Continuing job losses in these sectors during 1985–90 are predicted but at the reduced rate of 8 per cent (Rajan and Pearson, 1986). In the sunrise industries, the traditional male blue-collar worker is increasingly being displaced by white-collar, female and part-time employees. Female employment is expected to rise from 45 to 50 per cent of the workforce, and part-time employment from 20 to 25 per cent of total employment between 1985 and 1990. Although the union membership of these groups has increased since the 1960s, they remain more difficult for unions to organise (Price and Bain, 1983).

7 A family-owned furniture manufacturer founded in 1947, Panache Upholstery, made satisfactory profits until 1977. Then problems of succession, declining markets and a series of poor management decisions resulted in company liquidation in August 1980. All 83 employees were made redundant. A management buyout with employee financial support re-employed 60 people in October 1980. (See Wright and Coyne, 1985: pp. 160–9.)

8 In autumn 1984, when British Telecom was privatised, three advantageous share schemes were made available to employees: (i) a free offer of 54 shares to any employee; (ii) for those employees who invested their own money, two shares were given for each one bought subject to a maximum of £300; and (iii) a 10 per cent discount was available for any other shares bought up to a maximum of £1,600.

9 Since the Transfer of Undertakings (Protection of Employment) regulations issued in 1981, it has become more difficult to engineer a buyout by creating a break in employment, this triggering the redundancy payments which could be invested in share purchase. These regulations were designed to protect employees from unfair dismissal on a change of ownership. Where this problem arises, it may be necessary to adjust the purchase price. The regulation does not affect buyout attempts where no break in employment occurs, i.e. from corporate divestitures.

10 Internalisation of capital need not be confined to the workforce. The effects of a plant closure may be felt by the wider local community. Bradley and Gelb (1983a) suggested that buyout conversions were more likely to occur where: (i) strong local community links existed; and (ii) the threatened plant was a key local employer. Plant closure would therefore have a negative multiplier effect

upon a community's trade and tax base, as the loss of employment generally reduces net incomes. Under these circumstances local government and community support may be mobilised. Their help may be crucial if employees are unable to raise the necessary capital on their own because of high capitalisation or no break in employment. In several cases local coalitions involving community traders, government agencies and employees have been formed. Strategies for revitalising entire local economies have also been attempted in the United States. The best-known case is the Jamestown Area Labor-Management Committee (JALMC), New York State. Composed of local government officials, managers and employees, the JALMC is charged with encouraging cooperative action to save jobs in plant closure situations, and with strengthening the economic base of the community. It provides training in new skills for workers and the creation of in-plant cooperative problem-solving projects (Whyte et al., 1983).

11 Since 1984, however, as the market in management buyouts has developed, the discount element of the sale price has been eroded by the success of the early publicised cases, the entry of new financiers into the capital market, shareholders' objections to discounted sales and the improved state of the economy.

12 Some of these plants were formally closed before the conversion to employee ownership.

13 Information may also include factors such as firm-specific expertise or good relationships with contractors, which external buyers may be denied.

14 Manual employees would of course have access to information through company accounts and returns to Companies House, but these data are often difficult to use and do not represent an informational advantage.

5 The employee investment decision at the NFC

1 BRS (Southern) is located in south-east England. In 1984 it operated out of 27 depots and a regional Head Office and employed some 1,150. In FY 1982–3, sales totalled £37 million with a net profit of £2.1 million. BRS (Southern) provides a wide range of road freight transport services, including contract hire, storage and distribution, truck rental and general haulage.

2 The questionnaire survey was undertaken at BRS (Southern). A random sample was taken from the firm's payroll which yielded 350 cases. Self-completing questionnaires were distributed to these individuals through the firm's internal mail during October 1984. One hundred and fifty-two usable questionnaires were returned. The general profile of respondents was compared with the rest of the company and appeared to be representative in terms of occupation, gender, age and length of service.

6 Employee ownership and industrial relations: issues

1 These hypotheses were consistent with the views of those behavioural scientists who stressed the need to align the goals and needs of the employees and the organisation as closely as possible. (McGregor, 1960; Argyris, 1964.)

2 Motivation is defined as an attitude towards job performance; the concept is based on a model developed by Vroom (1964) and Lawler (1973).

3 Rhodes and Steers' definition of organisational commitment was broader than Long's (1978a). It was based on Mowday, Steers and Porter's (1979) construct of (i) a strong desire to remain a part of the organisation; (ii) a willingness to exert high levels of effort on behalf of the organisation; and (iii) a belief in the values and goals of the organisation. But there is a good deal of overlap between this definition of organisational commitment and Long's definition of organisational identification, although the former is easier to operationalise.

4 In reality of course the wage system is more complex than a simple fixed wage element. In most British firms, employees' total remuneration includes a number of items other than the fixed-wage basic pay, such as fringe benefits, overtime payments, shift work allowance and forms of incentive payment schemes, all of which may fluctuate with firm performance. Moreover, many employees are already paid a share of the value of their output, including the self-employed and commission agents.

5 Weitzman demonstrated the mechanism at the level of the individual firm. A typical capitalist firm hires labour until the marginal product of labour equals total pay. In a remuneration system that combines basic pay and profit-sharing, firms hire workers until the marginal product of labour equals the basic wage, because each additional worker employed down to the basic wage contributes to the non-labour share of profits. If, as Weitzman assumed, the basic wage could be set sufficiently low for labour demand to exceed full employment at every feasible level of aggregate demand, the share economy would create an excess demand for labour.

6 If the employees' share of profits is determined after any new investments, then employees will lose immediate income. This may be unacceptable to those approaching retirement, who might receive no income benefits from new investment, and also to those who prefer immediate income to the possibility of a higher future income. Furthermore, if the employees' share of profits is determined before the new investment, then investors may reallocate funds because the return on their investment may be insufficient.

7 This assumption led early scientific management theorists to dismiss profit-sharing and employee share schemes as ineffective. Such schemes, it was argued, usually made only a small contribution to an employee's total remuneration; their incentives were less effective than those of individual-based schemes which linked profits and rewards more closely; moreover they encouraged shirking.

8 Empirical analysis of the macro-economic effects of employee financial participation, and in particular, Weitzman's share economy model, has proceeded more slowly. Perhaps the closest example is that of Japan which Weitzman himself has adduced as a successful case of share economy. In the post-war period Japanese corporations regularly paid bonuses varying between 15 to 20 per cent of total earnings. During the same period Japan also experienced relatively lower levels of unemployment and rapid economic growth. Hence the conclusion: 'that the only industrial economy in the world with anything

remotely resembling a share system should also display all the broad tendencies predicted by the theory strikes me as too much of a coincidence to write off entirely to cultural determinism' (Weitzman, 1984: p. 76).

However, a full analysis of Weitzman's evidence lies beyond the scope of this study (Wadhwani, 1985). As his theories cannot generally be tested at the macro-economic level, tests have focused on the micro-economic level, and the dynamics of the revenue- or profit-sharing firm. The experiment of the 15,000 fishermen in Britain who take a proportion (sometimes 100 per cent) of their remuneration in revenue-sharing schemes, resembles a share economy at the sectoral level. Revenue-sharing does appear to produce improved motivation and greater identification with the firm. Furthermore, employment was retained during recession although it is not clear whether revenue-sharing creates new employment. The fishermen's experience tends to vindicate Weitzman's theory during recession (Job Ownership Ltd, 1986b).

9 Since this study is concerned with the effects of employee ownership in corporate models with individual employee share ownership, the empirical literature on cooperative models of employee ownership should be viewed with caution. However, some producer cooperatives bear a close resemblance to the NFC model of employee ownership because they have individual rather than common share ownership. In the United States, the main examples are the plywood cooperatives in the north-west and the refuse-collecting scavenger cooperatives in San Francisco; in Europe there is the Mondragon system of cooperatives. (Berman, 1967; Bellas, 1972; Russell, 1985: Bradley and Gelb, 1983b.)

10 See Chapter 7 for a fuller discussion of this point.

11 The almost unanimous view that profit-sharing should not be viewed as a substitute for an adequate wage or salary has ominous implications for plans to link a high proportion of an employee's total remuneration to company profits as a means of providing wage flexibility, creating employment or improving productivity.

7 The effects of employee share ownership on industrial relations at the NFC

1 Drivers' unions resisted new productivity schemes which culminated in a major drivers' strike in 1960.

2 Regulation began with vehicle licensing in 1930, followed by a 'fair wages' clause in the Road and Rail Traffic Act 1933 which was the foundation of a modest form of wage regulation throughout the industry. The 1933 Act also laid down that the Industrial Court should take account of Joint Industrial Council agreements, or voluntary agreements, in deciding what constituted a 'fair wage' in road haulage. Furthermore, the Road and Rail Traffic Act 1933 limited the number of hours a driver could be at the wheel each day. Enforcement remained problematic, however, because of the fragmentation of the industry.

In terms of the three licence categories introduced in the 1933 Act, the 'fair wages' clause was easier to enforce in 'A' and 'B' licence hauliers, which covered public service transport and local private transport on short distance work. However, the 'C' licences, the private carriers, comprised approximately 80 per cent of all licensees. Furthermore, manufacturers could choose whether to transport in their own vehicles, or contract 'A' and 'B' licences. The new regulation encouraged manufacturers to shift from contracting hauliers to taking out their own 'C' licences, making it even more difficult to implement the 'fair wages' clause.

In 1934 a national conciliation board was set up to enforce the fair wage provisions where no voluntary agreements had been reached, and to encourage employees to participate in voluntary negotiations. However, the employers' association on the Board represented only 25 per cent of firms with 'A' and 'B' licence vehicles. Union participation was a little better. In 1938 the Road Haulage Wages Act made two major changes. Firstly, it replaced voluntary regulation of wages and conditions by statutory regulation through Central and Area Wages Boards. Secondly, 'C' licence holders were included under the regulations for the first time. Regulation was extended during the war when the Road Haulage Organisation controlled the road haulage network. Following the war, the Wages Council Act 1945, *inter alia*, converted the Road Haulage Wages Board into a Wages Council as long as voluntary machineries remained absent. The Council included representatives of employers, labour and the State. It would make recommendations on a wider range of issues than was permitted under the Wages Board, including guaranteed wages; if accepted, its recommendations would be enforced by the minister using Orders of Parliament.

3 A productivity scheme was first introduced in 1957 following the increase in the speed limit to 30 mph for lorries over 3 tons unladen weight. In 1965 a new speed limit again resulted in rescheduling. In 1968 another productivity deal provided scheduling at 40 mph and also increased flexibility of duties.

4 An early indication of the drivers' frustrations was a major unofficial strike in May 1951 by some 10,000 drivers in the south-east. In an attempt to introduce some order into BRS' activities, the Road Haulage Executive had introduced patrols to monitor drivers' routes, parking practices, speeding, etc. The drivers objected strongly to this 'spying' on their practices. The unions argued that the measures had been introduced unilaterally and they were eventually withdrawn after government intervention.

5 Wright and Coyne (1985) argue that a management buyout may give management the opportunity to restructure industrial relations, perhaps to make the institutions and processes more firm-specific. In their survey, firms recognising trade unions declined by 8 per cent post-buyout, but there was little evidence to suggest that union removal was a management objective. Similarly the reduced prevalence of closed shops post-buyout does not appear to have been the outcome of management opposition.

6 Kruse (1984) found that 75 per cent of union respondents perceived a greater need for trade union representation after the introduction of Employee Stock Ownership Plans. The key issue may have been representation. The two ESOPs

he studied did not include voting rights, so that union remained the only significant way for workers to influence decisions. (See Kruse, 1984: p. 133.)

7 The five-week national road haulage strike in early 1979, for example, did not officially involve the NFC, although unofficial action and secondary picketing had damaging effects in some areas, with a total cost to the NFC of about £5 million.

8 For a detailed account of the scavenger cooperatives, see Russell (1985).

9 Economically, one might argue that three groups have been created at the NFC: shareholders receiving tax relief on interest; shareholders not receiving tax relief; and non-shareholders. See Chapter 5.

10 A Likert scale is a five-point discrete scale on which each point represents a strength of opinion. Table 7.5 uses Likert scales and coefficients are expressed as means. The range used in this case is as follows: 1 Great extent; 2 Some extent; 3 Don't know; 4 Not very much; 5 Not at all. Therefore, the lower the mean the higher the perception of share ownership. However, to be consistent, in the discussion of the table in the text, we employ percentages.

References

Alchian, A. A. and Demsetz, H. (1972), 'Production, Information Costs, and Economic Organization', *American Economic Review*, Vol. 62, No. 5, December, pp. 777–95.

Argyris, C. (1964), *Integrating the Individual and the Organisation*, Wiley, New York.

Arnfield, R. V., Chiplin, B., Wright, M. and Jarrett, M. G. (1981), *Management Buyouts: Corporate Trend for the 80s?* Department of Industrial Economics, University of Nottingham, Nottingham.

Bacon, R. and Eltis, W. (1978), *Britain's Economic Malaise: Too Few Producers*, 2nd edn, Macmillan, London.

Bassett, P. (1986), *Strike Free: The New Industrial Relations in Britain*, Macmillan, London.

Beesley, M. and Littlechild, S. (1983), 'Privatization: Principles, Problems and Priorities', *Lloyds Bank Review*, No. 149, July, pp. 1–20.

Bellas, C. (1972), *Industrial Democracy and the Worker Owned Firm: A Study of 21 Plywood Companies in the Pacific North West*, Praeger, New York.

Bendix, R. (1963), *Work and Authority in Industry*, Harper and Row, New York.

Berman, K. V. (1967), *Worker Owned Plywood Companies: An Economic Analysis*, Washington State University Press, Pullman.

Bevan, R. G. (1980), 'Cash Limits', *Fiscal Studies*, Vol. 1, No. 4, November, pp. 26–43.

Blanchflower, D. G. and Oswald, A. J. (1986a), 'Shares for Employees: A Test of their Effects', London School of Economics, mimeo, May.

(1986b), *Profit Related Pay: Prose Discovered?* New Bridge Street Consultants Ltd, London, October.

Bluestone, B. and Harrison, B. (1982), *The Deindustrialization of America*, Basic Books, New York.

Bradley, K. and Estrin, S. (1986), 'The Success Story of the John Lewis Partnership: A Study of Comparative Performance', Partnership Research Ltd, London, September.

(1988), 'Profit Sharing in the Retail Trade Sector: The Relative Importance of the John Lewis Partnership', Centre for Labour Economics Discussion Paper No. 279, London School of Economics.

Bradley, K. and Gelb, A. (1983a), *Worker Capitalism: The New Industrial Relations*, Heinemann Educational, London.

(1983b), *Co-operation at Work: The Mondragon Experience*, Heinemann Educational, London.

(1985), 'Employee Buyouts of Troubled Companies', *Harvard Business Review*, September/October, pp. 121–30.

(1986), *Share Ownership for Employees*, Public Policy Centre, London.

(1987), 'Cooperative Industrial Relations: Mondragon's Experience Over Recession', *British Journal of Industrial Relations*, Vol. 25, No. 1, pp. 77–98.

Bradley, K. and Hill, S. (1983), 'After Japan: The Quality Circle Transplant and Productive Efficiency', *British Journal of Industrial Relations*, Vol. 21, No. 3, November, pp. 291–310.

(1987), 'Quality Circles and Managerial Interest', *Industrial Relations Journal*, Berkeley, Cal., Vol. 26, No. 1, pp. 68–82.

British Transport Commission (1950), 'Integration of Services by Road and Rail: A Statement of Policy', July.

Brittan, S. (1984), 'The Politics and Economics of Privatisation', *Political Quarterly*, Vol. 55, No. 2, April/June, pp. 109–28.

Brooks, L. D., Henry, J. B. and Livingston, D. T. (1982), 'How Profitable Are Employee Stock Ownership Plans?' *Financial Executive*, May, pp. 32–40.

Brown, W. (ed.) (1981), *The Changing Contours of British Industrial Relations: A Survey of Manufacturing Industry*, Basil Blackwell, Oxford.

Bullock, A. (1960), *The Life and Times of Ernest Bevin*, Volume 1, Heinemann, London.

Bullock Report, See: Report of the Committee of Inquiry...

Cable, J. R. and Fitzroy, F. R. (1980a), 'Productive Efficiency, Incentives and Employee Participation: Some Preliminary Results for West Germany', *Kyklos*, Vol. 33, No. 1.

(1980b), 'Co-operation and Productivity: Some Evidence from the West German Experience', in A. Clayre (ed.), *The Political Economy of Co-operation and Participation*, Oxford University Press, Oxford, pp. 141–60.

Chisholm, M. (1959), 'Economies of Scale in Road Goods Transport? Off-Farm Milk Collection in England and Wales', *Oxford Economic Papers*, Vol. 11, No. 3, October, pp. 282–90.

Clayre, A. (ed.) (1980), *The Political Economy of Co-operation and Participation*, Oxford University Press, Oxford.

Coase, R. (1937), 'The Nature of the Firm', *Economica*, Vol. 4 (New Series), November, pp. 386–405.

Coates, K. (ed.) (1976), *The New Worker Co-operatives*, Institute of Workers' Control, Spokesman Books, Nottingham.

Conservative Party (1979), *The Conservative Manifesto*, Conservative Central Office, London, April.

Conte, M. (1982), 'Participation and Performance in US Labor Managed Firms',

List of references

in D. C. Jones and J. Svejnar (eds.), *Participatory and Self-Managed Firms*, Lexington Books, Lexington, Mass., pp. 213–37.

Co-operative Development Agency (1986), *Annual Report and Accounts*.

Copeman, G., Moore, P. and Arrowsmith, C. (1984), *Shared Ownership*, Gower, London.

Copeman Paterson (1986), *Employee Share Schemes*, Wider Share Ownership Council.

Cosh, A., Hughes, A. and Singh, A. (1980), 'The Causes and Effects of Takeovers in the United Kingdom: An Emiprical Investigation for the Late 1960s at the Microeconomic Level', in D. C. Mueller (ed.), *The Determinants and Effects of Mergers*, Oelgeschlager, Gunn and Hain, Boston, Mass., pp. 227–70.

Coyne, J. and Wright, M. (1982a), 'Staff Buyouts and the Privatisation of Nationalised Industries', Discussion Papers in Industrial Economics, Department of Industrial Economics, Nottingham University, May.

(1982b), 'Buyouts and British Industry', *Lloyds Bank Review*, No. 146, October, pp. 15–31.

Crosland, C. A. R. (1956), *The Future of Socialism*, Cape, London.

Dahl, R. A. (1970), *After the Revolution: Authority in a Good Society*, Yale University Press, New Haven, Connecticut.

Daniel, W. W. (1974), 'A National Survey of the Unemployed', PEP, Broadsheet No. 546, October.

Daniel, W. W. and Millward, N. (1983), *Workplace Industrial Relations in Britain*, DE/PSI/SSRC Survey, Heinemann Educational, London.

Department of Employment (1987), 'Membership of Trade Unions in 1985', *Employment Gazette*, Vol. 95, No. 2, February, pp. 84–6.

Donovan Commission (1968), See: Royal Commission.

Du Cann, E. (1984), 'Preface', in Institute of Directors, *Share Ownership for Employees and Directors*, Institute of Directors, Pall Mall, London, February.

Eccles, T. (1981), *Under New Management*, Pan Books, London.

Economist (1978), 'Appomatox or Civil War?' 27 May–2 June, pp. 21–2.

Economist Intelligence Unit (1984), 'Management Buy-Outs', 2nd edn, Special Report No. 164, Economist Intelligence Unit Ltd, London, March.

Estrin, S. (1985), 'The Role of Producer Cooperatives in Employment Creation', Paper presented to the Fourth International Conference on the Economics of Self-Management, Liège, Belgium, 15 July.

Estrin, S., Jones, D. C. and Svejnar, J. (1984), 'The Varying Nature, Importance and Productivity Effects of Worker Participation: Evidence from Contemporary Westen Industrialised Economies', unpublished, mimeo.

Estrin, S. and Wilson, N. (1986), 'The Micro-Economic Effects of Profit-Sharing: The British Experience', Centre for Labour Economics Discussion Paper No. 247, London School of Economics.

Financial Times (1986), 'Surge in Individual Share-ownership', 26 June.

Financial Times Survey (1981), 'Management Buy-Outs', October.

Financial Weekly (1986), 'Unions Ain't What They Used To Be', No. 402, 4 December, pp. 26–32.

Foster, N., Henry, S. G. B. and Trinder, C. (1984), 'Public and Private Sector Pay: A Partly Disaggregated Study', *National Institute Economic Review*, No. 107, February, pp. 63–73.

Fowler, N. (1977), 'The Right Track – A Paper on Conservative Transport Policy', Conservative Political Centre, London, September.

Freeman, R. B. and Medoff, J. L. (1984), *What Do Unions Do?* Basic Books, New York.

Friedman, M. (1962), *Capitalism and Freedom*, University of Chicago Press, Chicago.

Gamson, W. A. (1968), *Power and Discontent*, Dorsey Press, Homewood, Illinois.

George, K. D. and Joll, J. (1981), *Industrial Organisation*, 3rd edn, Allen and Unwin, London.

Goldstein, S. G. (1978), 'Employee Share-Ownership and Motivation', *Journal of Industrial Relations*, Vol. 20, No. 3, September, pp. 311–30.

Goodman, G. (1979), *The Awkward Warrior*, Davis-Poynter, London.

Green Paper (1986), *Profit Related Pay: A Consultative Document*, Cmnd 9835, HMSO, London, July.

Hammer, T. H. and Stern, R. (1980), 'Employee Ownership: Implications for the Organisational Distribution of Power', *Academy of Management Journal*, Vol. 23, No. 1, pp. 78–100.

Harrigan, K. R. (1980), *Strategies for Declining Businesses*, Lexington Books, D. C. Heath, Lexington, Mass. and Toronto.

Hart, P. E. (1953), 'The Efficiency of the Road Haulage Industry Under Nationalisation', *Journal of Industrial Economics*, Vol. 2, No. 1, November, pp. 51–7.

Hayek, F. A. (1944), *The Road to Serfdom*, Routledge, London.

Heald, D. (1983), *Public Expenditure: Its Defence and Reform*, Martin Robertson, Oxford.

Heald, D. and Steel, D. (1982), 'Privatising Public Enterprise: An Analysis of the Government's Case', *Political Quarterly*, Vol. 53, No. 3, July/September, pp. 333–49.

Hollowell, P. G. (1968), *The Lorry Driver*, Routledge & Kegan Paul, London.

Howe, G. (1981), 'Privatisation: The Way Ahead', Conservative Political Centre, London, August.

Incomes Data Services (1986), 'Profit Sharing and Share Options', IDS Study No. 357, London, March.

Industrial Relations Review and Report (1984), 'Bargaining for Survival at Eastern Air Lines', No. 319, 8 May.

Jackman, R. (1985), 'Professor Weitzman and the Unions, or Why Profit Sharing is Just Another Form of Wage Tax: A Note', Centre for Labour Economics, mimeo, August.

Jay, P. (1980), 'The Workers' Co-operative Economy', in A. Clayre (ed.), *The Political Economy of Co-operation and Participation*, Oxford University Press, Oxford, pp. 9–45.

Jensen, M. C. and Meckling, W. H. (1979), 'Rights and Production Functions: An Application to Labor-Managed Firms and Co-determination', *Journal of Business*, Vol. 4, October, pp. 469–506.

List of references

Job Ownership Ltd (1986a), 'A Neat Exit: The Transformation of French Family Businesses into Co-operatives', Partnership Research Ltd, London, September.

(1986b), 'The Share Economies in Britain's Inshore Fishing Fleet and in Coastal Shipping', Partnership Research Ltd, London, September.

Johannesen, J. (1979), 'VAG: A Need for Education', *Industrial Relations*, Vol. 18, No. 3, pp. 364–9.

Jones, D. C. and Svejnar, J. (1985), 'Participation, Profit Sharing, Worker Ownership and Efficiency in Italian Producer Co-operatives', *Economica*, Vol. 52, No. 208, November, pp. 449–65.

Joseph, K. (1975), 'Why Britain Needs a Social Market Economy', Centre for Policy Studies, Chichester.

Kay, J. A. and Silberston, Z. A. (1984), 'The New Industrial Policy – Privatisation and Competition', *Midland Bank Review*, Spring, pp. 8–16.

Kelf-Cohen, R. (1973), *British Nationalisation 1945–1973*, Macmillan, London.

Kornai, J. (1980), *The Economics of Shortage*, North-Holland, Amsterdam.

Kruse, D. (1984), *Employee Ownership and Employee Attitudes: Two Case Studies*, Worker Ownership and Participation Book Series, Vol. 1, Norwood Edition.

Labour Research Department (1983), '*Privatisation: Who Loses Who Profits?*' Labour Research Department Publications, London, May.

(1985), Privatisation: The Great Sellout', Labour Research Department Publications, London, February.

Lawler, E. E. (1973), *Motivation in Work Organisations*, Brooks and Cole, Monterey, Cal.

Leibenstein, H. (1966), 'Allocative Efficiency vs X-Efficiency', *American Economic Review*, Vol. 56, No. 3, June, pp. 392–415.

Letwin, O. (1988), *Privatising the World*, Cassell Educational, London.

Levin, H. (1982), 'Issues in Assessing the Comparative Productivity of Worker-Managed and Participatory Firms in Capitalist Societies', in D. C. Jones and J. Svejnar (eds.), *Participatory and Self-Managed Firms*, Lexington Books, Lexington, Mass., pp. 45–64.

Livingston, D. T. and Henry, J. B. (1980), 'The Effect of Employee Stock Ownership Plans on Corporate Profits', *Journal of Risk and Insurance*, Vol. 47, pp. 491–505.

Lloyd, P. A. (1976), *Incentive Payment Schemes*, Management Survey Report No. 34, British Institute of Management, London.

Lockett, M. (1981), 'Workers Co-operatives as an Alternative Organisational Form: Incorporation or Transformation?' in D. Dunkerley and G. Salaman (eds.), *International Yearbook of Organisational Studies*, Routledge and Kegan Paul, London, pp. 172–96.

Long, R. J. (1978a), 'The Effects of Employee Ownership on Organizational Identification, Employee Job Attitudes, and Organisational Performance: A Tentative Framework and Empirical Findings', *Human Relations*, Vol. 31, No. 1, January, pp. 29–48.

(1978b), 'The Relative Effects of Share Ownership vs Control on Job Attitudes in an Employee-Owned Company', *Human Relations*, Vol. 31, No. 9, September, pp. 753–63.

(1979), 'Employee Ownership and Attitudes Towards the Union', *Relations Industrielles*, Vol. 33, No. 2, pp. 237–54.

(1980), 'Job Attitudes and Organizational Performance Under Employee Ownership', *Academy of Management Journal*, Vol. 23, No. 4, December, pp. 726–37.

(1981), 'The Effects of Formal Employee Participation in Ownership and Decision-Making on Perceived and Desired Patterns of Organisational Influence: A Longitudinal Study', *Human Relations*, Vol. 34, No. 10, November, pp. 847–76.

(1984), 'The Effects of Employee Ownership on Job Attitudes and Organisational Performance: An Overview of the Empirical Literature', Paper presented at the National Employee Ownership and Participation Conference for Educators, Greenboro, N.C., October.

Lumby, S. (1981), 'New Ways of Financing Nationalized Industries', *Lloyds Bank Review*, No. 141, July, pp. 34–44.

McGregor, D. (1960), *The Human Side of Enterprise*, McGraw-Hill, New York.

MacKay, D. I. and Reid, G. (1972), 'Redundancy, Unemployment and Manpower Policy', *Economic Journal*, Vol. 82, No. 328, December, pp. 1256–72.

McLachlan, S. (1983), *The National Freight Buy-Out*, Macmillan, London.

Mann, M. (1985), 'Socialism Can Survive: Social Change and the Labour Party', *Fabian Tract No. 502*, Fabian Society, London, March.

Manwaring, T. and Sigler, N. (eds.) (1985), *Breaking the Nation: A Guide to Thatcher's Britain*, Pluto Press, London.

Marsh, T. and McAllister, D. (1981), 'ESOPs Fables: A Survey of Companies with Employee Stock Ownership Plans', *Journal of Corporation Law*, Vol. 6, No. 3.

Meade, J. E. (1986), *Different Forms of Share Economy*, Public Policy Centre, London.

Meeks, G. (1977), 'Disappointing Marriages: A Study of the Gains from Mergers', Department of Applied Economics Occasional Paper No. 51, University of Cambridge.

Millward, N. and Stevens, M. (1986), *British Workplace Industrial Relations 1980–1984* (DE/ESRC/PSI/ACAS Surveys), Gower, Aldershot.

Millward, R. (1982), 'The Comparative Performance of Public and Private Ownership', in Lord Roll of Ipsden (ed.), *The Mixed Economy*, Macmillan, London.

Moore, J. (1983), 'Why Privatise?' Speech reprinted in J. Kay, C. Mayer and D. Thompson (eds.) (1986), *Privatisation and Regulation: The UK Experience*, Clarendon Press, Oxford, pp. 78–94.

(1984), 'A People's Capital Market', Share Options and Incentives Conference, Institute of Directors, 5 December.

Morrison, H. (1933), *Socialisation and Transport*, Constable, London.

Mowday, R. T., Steers, R. M. and Porter, L. W. (1979), 'The Measurement of Organizational Commitment', *Journal of Vocational Behaviour*, Vol. 14, pp. 224–47.

List of references

Mueller, D. C. (ed.) (1980), *The Determinants and Effects of Mergers*, Oelgeschlager, Gunn and Hain, Boston, Mass.

National Freight Consortium plc, Report and Accounts, 1987, 1986, 1985, 1984, 1983, 1982.

National Freight Corporation (1977), 'Keeping Our People Informed', February.

Newman, K. (1986), *The Selling of British Telecom*, Holt, Rinehart and Winston, London.

Nickell, S. J. (1979), 'The Effect of Unemployment and Related Benefits on the Duration of Unemployment', *Economic Journal*, Vol. 89, March, pp. 34–49.

(1980), 'A Picture of Male Unemployment in Britain', *Economic Journal*, Vol. 90, December, pp. 796–4.

Nove, A. (1973), *Efficiency Criteria for Nationalised Industries*, Allen and Unwin, London.

Oakeshott, R. (1978), *The Case for Workers Co-ops*, Routledge and Kegan Paul, London.

Pauley, R. (1984), 'Mr Lawson's £10bn Balancing Act', *Financial Times*, 7 February, p. 16.

Peacock, A. and Shaw, G. K. (1981), 'The Public Sector Borrowing Requirement', Occasional Papers in Economics No. 1, University College at Buckingham.

Perotin, V. and Estrin, S. (1986), 'Does Ownership Matter?' London School of Economics, mimeo, July.

Pickering, C. (1984), 'The Mechanics of Disposal', in D. Steel and D. Heald (eds.), *Privatizing Public Enterprises: Options and Dilemmas*, Royal Institute of Public Administration, London, pp. 45–58.

Pliatzky, L. (1985), 'Who Owns the Publically Owned Industries?' *Policy Studies*, Vol. 5, Part 3, January, pp. 46–51.

Poole, M. (1975), *Workers' Participation in Industry*, Routledge and Kegan Paul, London.

Price, R. and Bain, G. S. (1983), 'Union Growth: Retrospect and Prospect', *British Journal of Industrial Relations*, Vol. 21, No. 1, March, pp. 46–68.

Pryke, R. (1971), *Public Enterprise in Practice*, MacGibbon and Kee, London.

(1981), *The Nationalised Industries*, Martin Robertson, Oxford.

(1982), 'The Comparative Performance of Public and Private Enterprise', *Fiscal Studies*, July, pp. 68–81.

Rajan, A. and Pearson, R. (eds.) (1986), *UK Occupation and Employment Trends to 1990*, Occupations Study Group, Institute of Manpower Studies, Butterworths, London.

Ramsay, H. (1977), 'Cycles of Control: Worker Participation in Sociological and Historical Perspective', *Sociology*, Vol. 11, No. 3, September, pp. 481–506.

Redwood, J. (1980), *Public Enterprise in Crisis*, Basil Blackwell, Oxford.

Redwood, J. and Hatch, J. (1982), *Controlling Public Industries*, Basil Blackwell, Oxford.

Reorganization of the Nationalized Transport Undertakings, Cmnd 1248, HMSO, London, 1960.

Report of the Committee of Inquiry on Industrial Democracy, Cmnd 6706, HMSO, London, January 1977.

Rhodes, S. R. and Steers, R. M. (1981), 'Conventional vs Workers-Owned Organisations', *Human Relations*, Vol. 34, No. 12, December, pp. 1013–37.

Richardson, R. and Nejad, A. (1986), 'Employee Share Ownership Schemes in the UK – An Evaluation', *British Journal of Industrial Relations*, Vol. 24, No. 2, July, pp. 233–50.

Riddell, P. (1983), *The Thatcher Government*, Martin Robertson, Oxford.

Road Haulage Operators' Licensing, Report of the Independent (Foster) Committee of Inquiry, HMSO, London, 1979.

Rothschild-Whitt, J. (1983), 'Workers' Ownership in Relation to Control: A Typology of Work Reform', in C. Crouch and F. Heller (eds.), *Organisational Democracy and Political Processes*, Wiley, London, pp. 389–405.

Royal Commission on Trade Unions and Employers' Associations Report, Cmnd 3623, HMSO, London, 1968.

Russell, R. (1985), *Sharing Ownership in the Workplace*, State University of New York Press, Albany.

Russell, R., Hochner, A. and Perry, S. E. (1979), 'Partnership, Influence, and Worker-Ownership', *Industrial Relations*, Vol. 18, No. 3, Fall, pp. 330–41.

Samuelson, P. A. (1977), 'Thoughts on Profit Sharing', in *Zeitschrift für die Gesamte Staastswissenschaft* (Special issue: Profit Sharing).

Shackleton, J. R. (1984), 'Privatization: The Case Examined', *National Westminster Bank Quarterly Review*, May, pp. 59–73.

Sharkey, W. (1982), *The Theory of Natural Monopoly* Cambridge University Press, Cambridge.

Smith, G. R. (1986), 'Profit Sharing and Employee Share Ownership in Britain', *Employment Gazette*, September, pp. 380–5.

Steel, D. (1984), 'Government and the New Hybrids', *Fiscal Studies*, Vol. 5, No. 1, February, pp. 87–97.

Steel, D. and Heald, D. (eds.) (1984), *Privatising Public Enterprises: Options and Dilemmas*, Royal Institute of Public Administration, London.

Stern, R. N. (1982), 'Trade Union Approaches to Employee Ownership in the US: Threats and Opportunities', Paper prepared for the EGOS meeting on Labour Unions, Florence, Italy, January.

Stern, R. N. and Hammer, T. H. (1978), 'Buying Your Job: Factors Affecting the Success or Failure of Employee Acquisition Attempts', *Human Relations*, Vol. 31, No. 12, December, pp. 1101–18.

Stern, R. N., Wood, K. H. and Hammer, T. H. (1979), *Employee Ownership in Plant Shutdowns: Prospects for Employee Stability*, Upjohn Institute for Employment Research, Kalamazoo, Michigan.

Tannenbaum, A. and Conte, M. (1976), 'Employee Ownership: Report to the Economic Development Administration', US Dept of Commerce Project Number 99-6-09433, Survey Research Center, University of Michigan, Ann Arbor, June.

Thomas, D. (1984), 'The Union Response to Denationalisation', in D. Steel and D. Heald (eds.), *Privatising Public Enterprises: Options and Dilemmas*, Royal Institute of Public Administration, London, pp. 59–76.

List of references

Thomas, H. and Logan, C. (1982), *Mondragon: An Economic Analysis*, Allen and Unwin, London.

Thomson, A. W. J. and Hunter, L. C. (1973), *The Nationalised Transport Industies*, Heinemann Educational, London.

The Times (1985), 'Stockton Attacks Thatcher Policies', 9 November, London.

Toscano, D. J. (1983), 'Toward a Typology of Employee Ownership', *Human Relations*, Vol. 36, No. 7, pp. 581–602.

Trades Union Congress (1974), 'Industrial Democracy: A Statement of Policy by the Trades Union Congress', TUC, London.

(1985), 'Stripping Our Assets: The City's Privatisation Killing', TUC, London, May.

(1986), 'Bargaining in Privatised Companies', TUC, London, February.

Transport Policy: A Consultation Document, HMSO, London, 1976.

Treasury, H. M. (1961), *The Financial and Economic Obligations of the Nationalised Industries*, Cmnd 1337, HMSO, London.

(1967), *Nationalised Industries: A Review of Economic and Financial Objectives*, Cmnd 1337, HMSO, London.

(1978), *The Nationalised Industries*, Cmnd 7131, HMSO, London.

(1980), *The Government's Expenidture Plans 1980–81 to 1983–84*, Cmnd 7841, HMSO, London.

(1981), *The Government's Expenditure Plans 1981–82 to 1983–84*, Cmnd 8175, HMSO, London.

(1982), *The Government's Expenditure Plans 1982–83 to 1984–85*, Cmnd 8494, HMSO, London.

(1983), *The Government's Expenditure Plans 1983–84 to 1985–86*, Cmnd 8789, HMSO, London.

(1984), *The Government's Expenditure Plans 1984–85 to 1986–87*, Cmnd 9143, HMSO, London.

(1986), *The Government's Expenditure Plans 1986–87 to 1988–89*, Cmnd 9702, HMSO, London.

Vanek, J. (1970), *The General Theory of Labour-Managed Market Economies*, Cornell University Press, Ithaca, New York, and London.

Veljanovski, C. (1987), *Selling the State*, Weidenfeld and Nicolson, London.

Vickers, J. and Yarrow, G. (1985), *Privatization and Natural Monopolies*, Public Policy Centre, London.

(1988), *Privatisation*, MIT, Cambridge, Mass.

Vroom, V. H. (1964), *Work and Motivation*, Wiley, New York.

Wadhwani, S. (1985), 'The Macroeconomic Implications of Profit Sharing: Some Empirical Evidence', Centre for Labour Economics Discussion Paper No. 220, London School of Economics, June.

Wadhwani, S. and Wall, M. (1988), 'The Effects of Profit-Sharing on Employment Wages, Stock Returns and Productivity: Evidence from UK Micro-Data', Centre for Labour Economics Discussion Paper No. 311, London School of Economics.

Wallace Bell, D. and Hanson, C. (1984), *Profit Sharing and Employee Shareholding*

Attitude Survey, Industrial Participation Association, November.

(1987), *Profit Sharing and Profitability*, Kogan Page, London.

Ward, B. (1958), 'The Firm in Illyria: Market Syndicalism', *American Economic Review*, Vol. 47, No. 4, September, pp. 566–89.

Webb, S. and B. (1897), *Industrial Democracy*, Longman, Green, London.

(1921), *Consumer's Cooperatives Movement*, Longman, Green, London.

Weitzman, M. L. (1984), *The Share Economy*, Harvard University Press, Cambridge, Massachusetts.

White Paper (1967), *The Transport of Freight*, Cmnd 3470, HMSO, London, November.

Whyte, W. H., Hammer, T. H., Meek, C. B., Nelson, R. and Stern, R. N. (1983), *Worker Participation and Ownership*, ILR Paperback Series No. 18, Cornell University, ILR Press, Ithaca, New York.

Williams, G. (1982), 'Management Buyouts', *The Accountant*, 18 March.

Winchester, D. (1983), 'Industrial Relations in the Public Sector', in G. S. Bain (ed.), *Industrial Relations in Britain*, Basil Blackwell, Oxford, pp. 155–78.

Woodworth, W. (1981), 'Forms of Employee Ownership and Workers Control', *Sociology of Work and Occupations*, Vol. 8, No. 2, May (Special issue, Economic Democracy: Comparative Views of Current Initiatives), pp. 195–200.

Wright, M. and Coyne, J. (1985), *Management Buy-Outs*, Croom Helm, London.

Yarrow, G. (1986), 'Privatization in Theory and Practice', *Economic Policy*, No. 2, April, pp. 323–78.

Zwerdling, D. (1978), *Democracy at Work*, Association for Self-Management, Washington, DC.

Index

Index

goods, 34, 38, 144–5; quality of, 33
government, 7, 12–13, 18, 24–7, 29–34,
    38–9, 44–51, 53–7, 59, 81, 97, 128,
    134, 140, 143–4, 146–8; a
    government's loss of receipts from
    profitable industries, 24; agencies,
    150; expenditure, 8; relationship
    between, and industry, 23;
    relationship between nationalised
    industries and, 22; the government's
    commitment: to fund the pensions
    deficiency, 53; to privatising the
    National Freight Corporation, 56;
    to sell council housing to tenants,
    144; (political), to the privatisation
    of the NFC, 53
growth, 34, 45, 134–5, 138; capital, 132;
    corporate, 14–15; economic, 14, 20,
    151; high, 15; low, 15; monetary,
    13, 23–4; long-term, 24

haulage, 145; activities, 85; general, 38, 41,
    48, 134, 145–6, 150; firms, 145;
    average size of, 146; units, 50;
    in-house, 132; meat, 145
haulier, 113, 144, 146; 'A' and 'B' licence,
    153; acquired, 37; contracting, 153;
    external, 38; external, specialist,
    132; private, 37–40, 85–6, 113,
    145–6; relative profitability of
    public- and private-sector, 41
· head office, 37, 50; personnel, 72; regional,
    150
home-owners, 68, 70, 80, 88

identification, 95, 99, 109; employee, with
    capital, 138; organisational 95, 151;
    (shareholders'), with the firm, 134,
    151
incentive, 1, 9, 15, 17, 30–1, 35, 52, 73,
    96–8, 110, 124, 126–7, 130, 151;
    economic, 98; financial, 110; for
    increased effort, 113; forms of
    incentive-payment schemes, 151;
    group, 98; incentive systems, 98;
    individual and associative, 98;
    individual financial, 98; diluted
    effects of the, 98; managerial, 23;
    non-financial, employee, 98; of
    ownership, 17, 66; perceptions of,
    125; performance-related, schemes,
    133; structure of, 109
incorporation, 48–9, 56–7; early, 33; late,
    33; phase, 148; relative autonomy
    of a lengthy, 57
independence, 17, 66, 85

industrial partnerships (*see* partnerships)
industrial relations, 1, 5–6, 8, 11, 25–6, 29,
    35, 92–3, 96–7, 100–1, 109–10,
    112–15, 117–18, 122, 129–30, 136–9,
    150, 153; actual impact on, 109;
    alternative models of, 1; conduct of,
    in the firm, 130; conventional
    academics, 139; harmonisation of,
    124; at the NFC, 112, 118;
    institutionalisation of, 144;
    institutions and processes of, 99;
    institutions for, regulation, 25; less
    harmonius, 115; macro-economic
    effects of improved, 97; main
    British, problem, 25; more
    co-operative, 109; policies, 144;
    predicted improvements in, 128;
    realism in, 139; specialists, x;
    substantive, issues, 138; traditional,
    2, 139; traditional, public-sector,
    138; workplace, 92
industry, 33, 36, 142; coal and steel, 28,
    142; concentration of, 14; declining,
    31, 35; (British) manufacturing, 1,
    106, 141; nationalised, 5–6, 18–20,
    22–3, 26, 29, 33–4, 36–8, 40, 52,
    134, 144; cash limits on the, 148;
    conventional funding arrangements
    of, 45; (productive) efficiency of the,
    9, 22; evaluation of the
    performance of, 20; inefficiencies of,
    27; insulation of the, from the
    financial markets, 22; performance
    of the, 143; peripheral activities of
    some British, 143; personnel from
    the, 46; potential inefficiency in, 21;
    relationship between, and
    government, 22; status of, 19;
    unpopularity of, 27; monopoly, 20;
    ownership of, 136; private, 47, 52;
    relationship between government
    and, 23; sunrise, 149; traditional,
    post-war, British, 8
inefficiency, 20, 22, 96; bureacratic, 22; in
    nationalised industries, 23;
    organisational, 100; potential, 21;
    productive, 21
inflation, 26, 131; inflationary forces,
    accumulation of, 2; price inflation,
    13, 43
information, 68–9, 77, 87, 90, 106, 122–3,
    133, 150; access to, 73; employees'
    access to external sources of, 82;
    greater access to, 88; alternative
    sources of, 84; communicating,
    downwards, 10; company

171

negotiation, 16–17, 25, 105, 117; national,
10; over pay and conditions, 10;
over the 'cash limits' of the EFLs,
144; pay, 117; successful purchase,
15; voluntary, 153; wage, 133; with
bidders, 147
North America, 8, 17, 66, 101

obligations: historical
obligations/liabilities, 147;
rail-based, 147; road-based, 147;
deficiencies on, 147; future,
unfunded, 147; non-historical, 147;
shortfall in the pension funds
arising from the, 147; rail-based
groups', 147; road-based groups'
147
occupation (JOB), 69, 82–3, 89–90, 150;
occupational group, 69, 72–3;
relationship between employee
ownership and occupation, 82;
relationship between employee
ownership and occupational group,
77
operations, 34, 67; level, 72, 128; operating
group, 134; units, 123, 130;
operational units, 133; increased
size of, 146
organisation, 8, 63, 95, 101, 129, 150–1;
capital-intensive, 32; cash-rich,
efficient and independent, 28;
economic performance of, 101;
employee-owned, 8;
labour–management relations in,
99; industrial, 138; internal control
of the, 93; mechanistic, 86; values
and goals of the, 151
output, 23, 98, 151; any one level of, 143;
per man hour, 41
owner, 4, 29, 113, 141; asset-stripping,
new, 49; employee-owners, 62, 92,
102; manager/managing, 85; new,
147; retiring, 142; worker-owners,
108
ownership (*see also* share ownership), 7,
10, 18, 20, 28, 31–2, 34, 62, 64,
92–4, 100, 106, 111, 123, 131, 138,
142, 149; blue-collar-employee, 77;
business, 142; change in, 26, 59, 68,
99–100, 122, 126–7, 130, 134;
employees' resistance to, 27;
collective, 102; of the means of
production, 63; common, 52;
community, 31; co-operative models
of, 94; distinction between
individual and social, 93;

distribution of, 7; environment,
changed, 93; equity, 3; forms of, 92;
corporate versus co-operative, 92;
individual versus collective, 92;
majority versus partial, 92; gap
between employee's expectations of,
and actual outcomes, 110; home,
79, 88, 137–8, 142; relationship
between employee home, and share,
88; individual, 93, 101, 141; of
capital, 19; joint-stock, 63;
manual-employee, 86; of British
industry, 5, 7; of productive assets,
6; of private-sector productive
assets, 139; optimal allocation of,
142; ownership stake, 18; private,
12–13, 19–20, 32; regulated private,
21; relative merits of common and
individual, 32; shareholder, 93;
shareholders' expectations from the
rights of, 111; shareholders' rights
of, 110; social 93, 141; state, 7, 32,
37; structure, changed, 95; structure
of, 139; new, 116; radical change in
the, 139; successful, 15; transfer of
5, 19, 21, 23, 26, 62;
white-collar-employee, 77
employee ownership, 1–2, 4–8, 11–12,
29, 31, 36, 62–4, 67, 69, 77–8, 81–5,
88, 92–5, 99–101, 103–4, 106,
108–11, 113–14, 116, 119–22, 124–6,
128–9, 133, 141, 144, 148, 150, 152;
conventional, 122; conversion to,
65, 99, 109, 115, 122, 150; debate,
92; different models of, 101; effects
of, 100, 152; effects of different
models of, on productivity, 95;
effects of, on performance, 101;
effects of the main form of partial,
102; effects of, on employee
attitudes, 138; on industrial
relations, 98, 109; on trade
unionism, 99; emergence of, 1, 140;
failure of some forms of, 100; high
level of, 135; majority, 9, 67, 94;
manual, 119; (NFC) model of, 93,
152; nature of, in Britain and the
United States, 141; negative
relationship between, and
productivity, 101; partial, 94, 101;
partial, scheme, 111; potential
consequences of, 94; precise nature
of, 109; privatisation and, 2;
relationship between, and age, 76;
relationship between, and depot
size, 86; relationship between, and